Timeless Tales
From Many Lands

ADVENTURE STORIES FOR TODAY'S KIDS

ILLUSTRATED BY JOHN MARDON
AND VESNA KRSTANOVICH

THE READER'S DIGEST ASSOCIATION, INC.
PLEASANTVILLE, NEW YORK/MONTREAL

A Reader's Digest Book

Acknowledgements

The publisher wishes to thank John Mardon and Vesna Krstanovich for graciously providing the artwork for this project. John Mardon: 8, 11, 13, 16, 27, 40, 56, 59, 82, 85, 87, 100, 106, 108, 124, 125, 155, 157, 160, 165, 168, 171, 173, 186, 189, 194, 197, 199, 208, 213, 214, 219, 220, 224, 225, 242, 244, 249, 251, 254, 262, 265, 269, 270, 276, 280, 293, 308, 322, 323, 328, 331, 333, 334. Vesna Krstanovich: 19, 21, 27, 28, 32, 35, 36, 42, 45, 51, 63, 64, 70, 72, 79, 90, 93, 97, 111, 113, 117, 122, 128, 133, 135, 138, 144, 150, 152, 176, 179, 182, 185, 200, 204, 206, 226, 232, 235, 237, 240, 242, 258, 274, 284, 287, 290, 296, 299, 313, 314, 315, 317.

READER'S DIGEST PROJECT STAFF

Project Editor:	Susan Randol
Contributing Design Director:	Jane Wilson
Editorial Manager:	Christine R. Guido

READER'S DIGEST ILLUSTRATED REFERENCE BOOKS

Editor-in-Chief:	Christopher Cavanaugh
Art Director:	Joan Mazzeo
Director, Trade Publishing:	Christopher T. Reggio
Senior Design Director, Trade:	Elizabeth L. Tunnicliffe

Library of Congress Cataloging in Publication Data

Timeless tales from many lands : adventure stories for today's kids / illustrated by John Mardon
and Vesna Krstanovich.
     p. cm.
Summary: A selection of tales from around the world, including Australia, East Africa, and Central America.
ISBN 0-7621-0339-6
1. Tales. [1. Folklore.] I. Mardon, John, ill. II. Krstanovich, Vesna, ill.

PZ8.1 .T4472 2001
398.2—dc21
2001019229

Printed in Spain

1 3 5 7 9 10 8 6 4 2

Contents

INTRODUCTION

What could be more wonderful, or more exciting, than to open the pages of a book and have the whole world spill out between your fingertips? In this collection of stories from far-away places and different times we have tried to do just that by offering tales from eighteenth century France, ancient Greece, Australia, ancient China, deepest Africa and sixteenth century India. All of these stories evoke a timeless sense of adventure and excitement and will fill even the most cautious temperament with a yearning for distant seas and far-away lands.

World literature is rich with folklore and culture. This treasury will lead you to some of the world's most interesting stories and tales. Open the covers and discover a faithful old friend or step beyond into a whole new adventure.

Visit Australia's outback, where Yael and Mulwarra avoid the gods by flying through the skies and finally diving into the sea for eternity. Explore ancient Mayan storytelling myths with the evil giants Earth-Mover and Earth-Shaker as they try to thwart the plan of the gods by destroying the Earth. Travel to East Africa, where if you are not careful, the spirits of the land will steal from your baskets and bewitch you if you disrespect them.

You'll also meet some memorable characters. There's France's Bluebeard, who keeps a mysterious door locked in his castle. There's Jack the Giant Killer, who stomps his way through the English moors beating any nasty giant that tries to interfere with him. There is an eccentric hare that manages to outwit a kingdom, and a family of beautiful young girls in China whose beauty could rival any flower.

Some of the worlds you will discover behind these stories are astonishing. What about a yellow horse and rider that save a family from drowning, just by dropping in for tea? Or a queen whose job it is to save her kingdom from darkness by appealing to the gods?

Whether astonishing, enlightening, or just downright enjoyable, these timeless tales will broaden your horizons and set your adventurous spirit sailing in the wind.

Puss in Boots

FRANCE

Once upon a time there was an aged miller who, when dying, left his property to his three sons, all he had being his mill, his donkey, and his cat.

An equal division of these was, of course, impossible, and to call in lawyers to try to do it would have eaten up the little there was, so the brothers wisely agreed that each should take a share as it stood, and make the best of it. The eldest son, therefore, got the mill; the second got the donkey; and only the cat was left for the youngest.

Very naturally he was grieved that his share was so small, and it puzzled him much to know what to do with it.

"My brothers," said he to himself, "can earn quite a decent living by working together—the one can grind the corn, and the other can carry it away in sacks when ground, but, as for me, even if I were to eat my cat and wear its skin, I might die of hunger afterward."

This speech made Puss, who was near, feel rather creepy, but he acted as if he had not overheard it, for he loved his master, who had always been kind to him, leaving him little bits of fish on the fish-bones he gave him, and letting him lie on his knee by the fire in the winter evenings.

With his tail in the air, he came forward and rubbed himself against his master's legs, purring his loudest to gain his attention;

then, as the young man stooped to stroke him, Puss looked up in his face and said cheerily:

"Do not lose heart, sir; just give me a bag with draw-strings and a pair of high boots to tramp through the briers with, and perhaps you will find that a cat may be worth more to you than *both* a mill and a donkey!"

His master did not build his hopes too high on hearing this speech, but he had often seen his cat's agility and cleverness in tricking the rats and mice—hanging head downward, as if dead, lying quite motionless among the meal, and suchlike—so he did not quite despair of being helped a little by Puss in his dire poverty.

When the cat got the things he asked for, he proudly drew on his boots, slung the bag round his neck, put a handful of bran and some lettuce leaves in it, took the strings in his forepaws, and went straight to one of the King's rabbit-warrens.

There he lay flat on the ground behind the bag, which he held open in front of him, and never moved till an unsuspecting young rabbit, smelling a good meal, crept into it. In a moment the strings were drawn tight—bunny was caught and killed. Another was enticed in the same way, and met the same fate.

Greatly pleased with his "bag," Puss set off for the palace, and asked to be allowed to speak to the King.

He was taken to his Majesty's apartment, where he made a low bow to the King, and said:

"Here, sir, is a pair of rabbits from the warrens of my lord, the Marquis of Carabas [this was the title he gave his master]. He has sent me to offer them to you, with his humble compliments."

"Tell your master from me," said the King, "that I thank him, and am pleased to accept his present."

On another occasion Puss went to hide in a field of wheat, his bag wide open as usual, and two unwary partridges ran into it.

These he also went to present to the King, who was again graciously pleased to receive them, and told his purser to give Puss some money for his trouble.

The cat continued to act in this way for several months, every few days carrying game to the King, and you may be sure that he kept his master well supplied also.

Hearing from the servants at the palace one day that the King and his daughter, the most beautiful princess in the world, were to take their drive along the road by the river, he said to his master:

"If you will take my advice, your fortune is made. You have only to go and bathe in the river, at the spot I shall show you, and leave the rest to me."

The young man did as his cat advised, though indeed he couldn't see what good it would do him.

Just as he was bathing the royal carriage passed, and the cat began to shout wildly: "Help! help!—the lord Marquis of Carabas is drowning!"

Hearing the cry, the King put his head out of the carriage-window, recognized the cat that brought him game so often, and at once ordered his guards to go to the assistance of his lordship the Marquis of Carabas.

Puss, in the meantime, had hidden his master's clothes under a heap of stones, and while the guards were helping our marquis out of the river, his cat, in a state of great excitement, ran toward the royal carriage and told the King that while his master, the marquis, was bathing, thieves had stolen his clothes and run off with them, though he had shouted "Stop, thief! Stop, thief!" at the top of his voice. Wherefore, though his master's life was saved, he had no clothes to put on.

His Majesty was greatly concerned to hear of the plight of the poor marquis, and he ordered two of his equerries to ride back post-haste to the palace, to fetch from the royal wardrobe the finest clothes they could find for his lordship.

A grand suit was soon brought and handed to the cat, who hastened with it to his master, and having helped him to dress in it, Puss conducted him to the royal carriage, to pay his grateful respects to the King and to thank his Majesty for such timely help.

The miller's son, being healthy and well built, was a good-looking young fellow at all times, but now, in his magnificent court dress, he looked so stately that few, if any, of the young nobles could compare with him.

The King, who had never seen the marquis till that day, was much struck with his handsome appearance.

He embraced him again and again, then presented him to his daughter, who had been watching the fine-looking young stranger with secret admiration.

His Majesty insisted that our marquis should join the royal party in their drive, and gave him the seat next to himself in the coach.

During the drive, while her father was talking to the marquis, the Princess could not help noticing the frequent glances of respectful admiration which his lordship of Carabas bestowed upon her, and before the drive was ended she had fallen deeply in love with him.

The cat, overjoyed to see his plans succeeding so well, now went on in front of the party, taking shortcuts wherever there was a bend in the road to keep ahead of the carriage.

Coming to some peasants who were mowing in a meadow by the roadside, he called to them:

"Listen, my good folk: the King is coming this way, and may ask you whose hay you are mowing. If he does, you must say it all belongs to his lordship the Marquis of Carabas. If you fail to say this, I shall have you all chopped into mince-meat."

As expected, the King stopped the carriage when it reached the meadow, and asked the peasants who was the owner of the hay they were cutting.

"It all belongs to his lordship the Marquis of Carabas," they shouted with one voice, remembering the cat's dreadful threat.

"That is a fine bit of meadow-land," said the King, turning to the marquis. "Yes, sire," he replied, "it yields a very heavy crop every year."

Master Puss, who always kept well ahead, next came to a band of reapers. "My good men," shouted he, "if you do not tell the King, who will pass shortly, that all the corn you are reaping belongs to the Marquis of Carabas, I shall have you all chopped into mince-meat."

The King, who passed shortly after, inquired to whom those splendid fields of wheat belonged.

"They belong to the Marquis of Carabas," the reapers all shouted together, and the King again congratulated the marquis.

The cat, who kept well on in front, gave the same directions to everyone whom he met, and as one and all were too terrified to disobey, the King was astonished at the great possessions of his new friend, the Marquis of Carabas.

Finally the cat came to a grand castle, and, on inquiry, he found that it and all the country through which they had driven belonged to an ogre, whose wealth was uncountable.

From the servants Puss found out all he could about this ogre, his riches, his power, his ferocity, and the many wonderful things he could do.

Then, saying he did not like to pass the castle without paying his respects to such a great person, he asked to see him.

The Ogre received the cat as politely as an ogre knows how to do, and asked him to rest a little while, and, if he had time, to stay to lunch with some friends whom he was expecting in a quarter of an hour.

The cat asked nothing better than the chance thus offered for carrying out his own plans.

"People tell me very wonderful things about your Highness," said the cat. "They even say that you can change your form when you like, and that you can turn yourself into a lion or an elephant at will. Is it so, really?"

"Certainly!" said the Ogre sharply. "And to satisfy you on that point I shall change myself into a lion." Which he did there and then.

No sooner did he see the lion before him than Puss jumped out of the window in terror, and, fearing pursuit, climbed up the gutter to the roof, not without both danger and difficulty, the boots being sadly in his way. These, though good for tramping over briers, were useless for clinging to slanting tiles.

When the Ogre had resumed his own form, Puss clambered down and re-entered by the window, frankly confessing that he had been dreadfully afraid.

"That *was* a feat!" said the cat; "but I have been told you can do a more wonderful one still. Is it true that you, who are so very big, can turn yourself as easily into quite a small animal like a rat or even a mouse? To my mind that would be quite impossible!"

"*Impossible!*" cried the Ogre scornfully. "You shall see!" A tiny mouse began to play on the floor! In a twinkling it was caught and eaten by the cat.

The royal party, by this time, had reached the castle, and the King made up his mind to call on the owner.

Puss heard the sound of the carriage on the drawbridge, and quickly went down to meet it. As it came through the gates, he made a sweeping bow to the King and said:

"Let me welcome your Majesty to the castle of his lordship the Marquis of Carabas."

"What! My lord Marquis," said the King, "this castle also is yours? Why, nothing could possibly be finer than this spacious courtyard and the noble buildings that surround it! Let us see the interior, if you please."

The Marquis gave his hand to the Princess to help her to alight, and they followed the King into the castle.

They entered the stately dining-hall, where they found the feast prepared for the Ogre's friends, who arrived at that moment, but who dared not go in when they heard that the King was there.

The servants, to whom the cat had given the hint, quickly helped the Marquis and his royal guests to all the good things on

the table—savory dishes, rich cakes, delicious ices, and the finest old wines from the Ogre's cellars.

The King and his daughter were not only charmed with the amiability and good looks of the Marquis, but also delighted to know of his wealth and great estates.

After having refreshed himself with a few glasses of wine, the King turned to his host and said: "My dear Marquis of Carabas, if you do not become my son-in-law, you will have yourself to blame!"

Our marquis rose and bowed low to the King, then turned to the Princess and, laying his hand on his heart, dropped on one knee before her.

With a pretty blush on her checks, the Princess got up from her seat and, holding out her hand, made him rise, and led him to her father, the King, who gave orders that their marriage should take place immediately.

Master Puss had been peeping and listening by the slightly open door of the room, hardly able to keep from mewing aloud with delight when he saw the turn things were taking; but now, when his hopes were crowned, he could hold himself no longer, and turned cartwheels from the top of the grand stair to the bottom in his joy.

The marriage was celebrated with great pomp and festivity, and the Marquis of Carabas and his bride lived happily to a good old age in the magnificent castle that had belonged to the Ogre.

The servants were delighted to have such a kind master and gentle mistress, for they had only served the Ogre from fear of what he might do to them.

The cat was made a great noble, and had part of the castle set apart for his own use.

Needless to say, he never again had to catch rats or mice, except for the pleasure of having a day's hunting!

The Monster with Emerald Teeth

MAYAN

It has been known, from time to time, that even the gods will make mistakes. There was the time when they first populated the earth with little men and women carved out of wood. But these carvings were so badly done, their very belongings rose up against them. They were stabbed by their knives, pecked by their chickens, and crushed by their houses. In the end, their millstones ground them to splinters.

The gods then decided to replace these little wood-men with giants. But these giants were really no better. Vukub-Cakix and his two sons, Earth-Mover and Earth-Shaker, were proud, vain, and cruel. Once the gods had created their masterpiece, humankind, the three giants made their lives miserable. The gods would have to get rid of them. But how?

In the end it was decided that the heavenly twins, Hun-Apu and Xbalanque, would go down to Earth and rid it of the three pesky giants. They flew at once to the nanze-tree where Vukub-Cakix picked his fruit each day. Hiding in the branches, they waited until Vukub had climbed to the very top of the tree before taking aim with their blowpipes.

"Owowo!" cried the giant, and fell to the ground, clutching his face. Though he had crashed like a meteorite, the fall did not kill him as Hun-Apu and Xbalanque had hoped. Rather, looking up into the tree he saw the two strangers, and with a ferocious snarl and gnashing of his emerald teeth, he came after them! Like lightning he was back in the tree and before the twins knew what was what, he grabbed Hun-Apu's arm and pulled it clean off of his body before the heavenly twins were able to escape.

"My arm!" said Hun-Apu after they'd stopped running. "I need it back! I can't go back to heaven without my arm!"

"Don't worry about that now," said Xbalanque. "Our giant friend has the most awful toothache. Our darts hit him right in the mouth."

"I'm not feeling too good myself," said his twin.

But they put on cloaks and masks and sought out the house of Vukub-Cakix, where his giantess wife, Chimalmat, was just getting ready to roast Hun-Apu's arm for dinner.

Terrible groans could be heard from the bedroom. The giant was in agony. "Oh! My teeth! Just when I reached the top of the tree it started," he told his wife. "If it hadn't been for that I'd have brought you home two thieves for dinner."

Just then the twins knocked upon the door:

"We were just passing when we heard the groans. We thought we might help, since we're dentists," they told Chimalmat.

She hurried them into her husband's room. Greenish light flickered from his emerald teeth as he lay writhing on the bed, swearing horribly.

"Say, 'aaaah,'" said Hun-Apu.

"Hmm. Just as I thought. All of your teeth are rotten. They will have to go," said Xbalanque, peering into the cavernous mouth.

"But his power!" whispered Chimalmat in awed tones. "All his strength and power are in his teeth! How will he bite off his enemies' heads? How will he grind their bones?"

"We shall give him a new set of teeth, naturally," said Xbalanque, and one by one he used his pliers to pull out the emerald teeth. An entire emerald mine would not have yielded so many jewels as were in Vukub-Cakix's mouth.

The new set of teeth Hun-Apu and Xbalanque gave to Vukub-Cakix were only bits of ground corn. And so, no more did the green light flicker upon the ceiling, and no more did Vukub's silvery eyes shine. He faded, faded, faded, like a fire going out in the night. Powerless, he watched the darkness close in upon him like a rising flood and carry his soul away.

"What about my arm?" asked Hun-Apu once the twins got outside. Xbalanque threw back his cloak and brandished the lost

limb he'd rescued from Chimalmat's fire. "A little magic," he said, "and you'll be as good as new." And so he was.

Next in line was Earth-Shaker, a braggart and a show-off. This would make him easy both to flatter and to find. They found him juggling three small mountains in the morning light.

"Wonderful!" cried the brothers, bursting into applause. "How clever! You must be very strong!"

Earth-Shaker looked down and smiled, pleased. "There is no mountain I cannot move. Show me one! I'll prove it!"

Xbalanque pointed to a far-distant snowcapped peak. "That one?"

"No problem," bragged the giant.

"First you must eat, what with all this pushing and juggling," suggested Hun-Apu. "Let me shoot you something to eat."

That was perfectly fine for Earth-Shaker, who was always hungry and busy devouring the wildlife tenderly placed by the gods. When a flock of macaws flew overhead, the twins put their blowpipes to their lips and brought down a pair of birds. They then smothered the birds in mud and baked them over a fire, presenting the feast to him. They did not tell them that the darts in their blowpipes were poisoned with curare, and that the mud they used to bake the birds was also poisonous. By the time Earth-Shaker had finished eating his meal, his head was spinning and his eyes were dim. He could barely see the mountain he was now supposed to move.

Nevertheless, Xbalanque and Hun-Apu led him there, ignoring his whimpers. "You can't do it, can you? You see, brother? He was just bragging," they said.

So Earth-Shaker, in his foolish pride, pushed against the mountain until his sweat ran down it in rivers. He pushed so hard his hands left prints that were a fathom deep. Finally his head burst with the strain of so much poison and so much showing off and he crumbled to the ground.

This left only Earth-Mover, proudest giant of them all.

Now Earth-Mover was very curious by nature. So to trap him, the twins decided to dig a massive pit that looked like the foundation of an enormous house, and then they waited. When Earth-Mover finally came alone, he immediately climbed down to inspect the pit. This could the beginning of a big house that he might just take for himself.

By the time that Earth-Mover saw the huge stack of tree trunks stacked beside the hole, it was too late. Xbalanque and Hun-Apu used crowbars to lever the huge logs forward and into the hole.

One by ten by hundreds, the huge tree trunks crashed into the pit on top of Earth-Mover. When the noise stopped, all was silent.

"Come one, come all, and build upon the ruins of the giants!" declared Xbalanque. "Build yourself a fine home over the broken bones of Earth-Mover; never again will you be bothered by his bullying!"

Four hundred young men came to do just that. They built a log house big enough for all of them to live in, and once it was built, there was an enormous celebration.

But beneath them, Earth-Mover was not dead, after all. He had found himself a crevice safe from the falling logs, and there he had bided his time, silver eyes gleaming, emerald teeth grinding. At midnight he got to his feet and, flinging up his great head, flinging out his huge arms, he tossed the house and its four hundred occupants into the night sky. It was like the eruption of a volcano.

So high were the young men thrown, so wide were their eyes with terror, that Xbalanque looked up and saw the moonlight glimmer in their eight hundred eyes. In that instant, he transformed the men into stars, to keep them from falling to their deaths.

Heartsick and angry, the heavenly twins worked alone to avenge the young men. They each cut through the bottom of two facing mountains, and when Earth-Mover walked through the valley between them, Xbalanque toppled one mountain on top of him and Hun-Apu toppled the other.

Like a blanket, the two mountains folded around the fallen giant. This time he must surely die! But then, out from between the boulders reached a hand, grasping and clawing. Then from the solid earth burst another! And so Xbalanque and Hun-Apu invoked the magic of the heavens, the magic of the gods that had made the giants a thousand years before.

Earth-Mover was turned to stone, petrified, stopped still and lifeless in the very act of grasping for life.

The Halloween Witches

AFRICAN AMERICAN

One Halloween night, when the moon didn't shine, some old witches got together in a cabin behind the dark pines. They sat round the fire cooking supper, telling tales about their friends and about the spells they would cast at midnight.

A good stranger came upon the cabin, and he knocked at the door.

The witches called, "Who's there? Who-oo? Who-oo?"

And a voice said, "A stranger. One who is hungry and cold."

They laughed and sang, "We're cooking for ourselves, we'll not cook for you!"

There was no reply, but the knocking kept on, steady and soft.

The witches took no notice and began to eat.

The knocking kept on, until the witches began to feel uneasy.

One of them said, "Let's give him something. He'll spoil our spells."

She took a tiny piece of dough, big as a pea, and set it on a pan on the stove. But as soon as the dough was on the pan it began to swell over the pan, over the stove, onto the floor.

The witches ran to the door. *But the door was shut tight.*

They jumped to the chairs. But still the dough swelled; it came over the chairs.

They climbed to the backs of the chairs and squished up as small as they could. Still the dough swelled.

The knocking stopped, and through the house came the words:

> *"You refuse to give, you refuse to lend;*
> *Criticize your neighbor, criticize your friend.*
> *Now hush your talking, hush your talk;*
> *You'll never more have strength to walk!"*

The witches' legs began to shrink. They were so surprised, they turned their heads right round, front to back. They were no longer witches. They were owls.

The dough had risen so high only a gap was left at the top of a window. The owls flew out into the woods, calling, "Who's that a-knocking? Who-oo? Who-oo?"

Even to this day, in the dark of night, owls fly calling, "Who-oo? Who-oo?"

Except at Halloween. On that night the owls turn back into witches and sneak about, weaving their wicked spells.

The Drovers Who Lost Their Feet

MEXICO

This is how the people from Lagos are. There were five drovers traveling together. They were tired. They sat down against a tree, and all of them stretched out their legs. They said, "What are we going to do? We won't be able to get up any more. We are no longer able to tell which of those feet belong to which. What are we going to do? We'll just have to stay here."

Whoo! There they were, pretty hungry and thirsty, and they couldn't get up.

A man passed by, and he said, "What are you doing there?"

"Well, here we are. We can't get up."

"Why?"

"Because we don't know which feet belong to which."

"For goodness' sake! How much will you give me if I tell you?"

"Well, we'll give you something, as long as you tell us which of those feet belong to which."

He took a big pack needle and began to stick them with it. He stuck one of them.

"Ouch!"

"That's yours. Pull it in."

He stuck another one of them.

"Ouch!"

"That's yours. That one. Pull it in."

And he stuck all of them the same way until he had the very last one on his feet.

Hansel and Gretel

GERMANY

O nce upon a time there dwelt on the outskirts of a large forest a poor woodcutter with his wife and two children; the boy was called Hansel and the girl Gretel. He always had little to live on, and once, when there was a famine, he couldn't even provide them with bread. One night, as he was tossing about, full of worry, he sighed and said to his wife: "What's to become of us? How are we to support our children, now that we have nothing more for ourselves?" "I'll tell you what, husband," answered the woman; "early tomorrow we'll take the children out into the thickest part of the woods; there we shall light a fire for them and give them each a piece of bread; then we'll go on to our work and leave them. They won't find their way home, and we shall be rid of them." "No, wife," said her husband, "how could I find it in my heart to leave my children in the woods? The wild beasts would come and tear them to pieces." "Oh! you fool," said she, "then we must all four die of hunger, and you may as well go and plane the boards for our coffins;" and she left him no peace till he consented. "But I can't help feeling sorry for the poor children," added the husband.

The children, too, had not been able to sleep for hunger, and had heard what their stepmother had said to their father. Gretel wept bitterly and spoke to Hansel: "Now it's all over for us." "No, no, Gretel," said Hansel, "don't fret; I'll find a way of escape, no fear." And when the old people had fallen asleep he got up, slipped on his coat, opened the back door, and stole out. The moon was shining, and the white pebbles that lay in front of the house glittered like bits of silver. Hansel bent and filled his pocket with as many as he could. Then he went back and said to Gretel, "Be comforted, my dear sister, and go to sleep. God will not desert us," and he lay down in bed again.

At daybreak, even before the sun was up, the woman came and woke the two children: "Get up, you lie-abeds, we're going to the forest to fetch wood." She gave them each a bit of bread and spoke: "There's something for your luncheon, but don't eat it now, for it's all you'll get." Gretel took the bread under her apron, as Hansel had the stones in his pocket. Then they all set out on the way to the forest. After they had walked for a little, Hansel stood still and looked back at the house. This he repeated again and again. His father observed him and spoke: "Hansel, what are you gazing at, and why do you remain behind? Take care, and don't lose your footing." "Oh! Father," said Hansel, "I am looking at my white kitten, sitting on the roof, waving me farewell." The woman exclaimed: "What a donkey you are! That isn't your kitten, that's the morning sun shining on the chimney." But Hansel had not looked back at his kitten, but had always dropped one of the white pebbles out of his pocket on to the path.

When they had reached the middle of the forest, the father said: "Now, children, go and fetch wood, and I'll light a fire so you won't feel cold." Hansel and Gretel heaped up brushwood till they had made a pile the size of a small hill. The brushwood was set fire to, and when the flames leaped high the woman said: "Now lie down at the fire, children, and rest. We are going into the forest to cut wood; when we've finished we'll come back and fetch you." Hansel and Gretel sat beside the fire, and at mid-day ate their bits of bread. They heard the strokes of the ax, so they thought their father was near. But it was no ax they heard, but a bough tied on to a dead tree that was blown about by the wind. And when they had sat for a time, their eyes closed, and they fell fast asleep. When they awoke it was pitch-dark. Gretel began to cry and said: "How are we ever to get out of the woods?" But Hansel comforted her. "Wait a bit," he said, "till the moon is up, and then we'll find our way." And when the full moon had risen he took his sister by the hand and followed the pebbles, which shone like new threepenny bits. They walked through the night, and at daybreak reached their father's house. They knocked at the door, and when the woman opened it she exclaimed: "You naughty children, what a time you've slept in the woods! We thought you were never going to come back." But the father rejoiced, for his conscience had reproached him for leaving his children behind.

Not long after there was again great dearth in the land, and the children heard their stepmother address their father thus in bed one night: "Everything is eaten up once more; we have only half a loaf in the house. The children must be got rid of; we'll lead them deeper into the woods this time, so that they won't be able to find their way out again. There is no other way." The man's heart smote him heavily, and he thought, "Surely it would be better to share the last bite with one's children!" But his wife wouldn't listen, and did nothing but scold and reproach him. If a man yields once he's done for, and so, because he had given in the first time, he was forced to do so the second.

But the children were awake and had heard the conversation. When the old people were asleep Hansel got up to go and pick up pebbles again, but the woman had barred the door. He consoled his little sister and said: "Don't cry, Gretel, and sleep peacefully, for God is sure to help us."

At early dawn the woman came and made the children get up. They received their bit of bread, but it was even smaller than before. On the way to the woods Hansel crumbled it in his pocket, and every few minutes he stood and dropped a crumb on the

ground. "Hansel, what are you stopping and looking about for?" said the father. "I'm looking back at my pigeon, sitting on the roof, waving me farewell," answered Hansel. "Fool!" said the wife, "that isn't your pigeon, it's the morning sun glittering on the chimney." But Hansel gradually threw all his crumbs on to the path. The woman led the children still deeper into the forest, further than they had ever been before. Then a big fire was lit again, and the woman said: "Sit, children, and if you're tired you can sleep; we're going into the forest to cut down wood, and in the evening we'll fetch you." At mid-day Gretel divided her bread with Hansel, for his was all along their path. Then they fell asleep, and evening passed, but nobody came to the poor children. They didn't awake till it was pitch-dark, and Hansel comforted his sister, saying: "Only wait, Gretel, till the moon rises, then we shall see the breadcrumbs I scattered along the path; they will show us the way back to the house." When the moon appeared they got up, but found no crumbs, for the thousands of birds that fly about the woods had picked them all up. "Never mind," said Hansel to Gretel, "you'll see we'll find a way out;" but they did not. They wandered about the whole night, and the next day, but could not find a path out of the woods. They were hungry, too, for they had nothing to eat but a few berries growing on the ground. And at last they were so tired that their legs refused to carry them any longer, so they lay down under a tree and fell fast asleep.

On the third morning after they had left their father's house, they set about wandering again, but only got deeper into the woods, and felt that if help did not come soon they must perish. At mid-day they saw a beautiful snow-white bird on a branch, which sang so sweetly that they stopped and listened to it. When its song was finished it flapped its wings and flew on in front of them. They followed and came to a little house, on the roof of which it perched; and when they came near they saw that the cottage was made of bread and roofed with cakes. The window was made of transparent sugar. "Now we're all set," said Hansel. "I'll eat a bit of the roof, and you can eat some of the window, which you'll find sweet." Hansel stretched his hand and broke off a bit of the roof to see what it was like, and Gretel went to the casement and began to nibble. Thereupon a shrill voice called from inside:

"Nibble, nibble, little mouse,
Who's nibbling my house?"

The children answered,

"'Tis Heaven's own child,
The tempest wild,"

and went on eating. Hansel, who thoroughly appreciated the roof, tore down a big bit of it, while Gretel pushed out a whole window-pane, and sat down to enjoy it. Suddenly the door opened and an ancient dame leaning on a staff hobbled out. Hansel and Gretel were so terrified that they let what they had in their hands fall. But the old woman shook her head and said: "Oh, ho! dear children, who led you here? Come in and stay with me; no ill shall befall you." She took them both by the hand and led them into the house, and laid a most sumptuous dinner before them—milk and sugared pancakes, with apples and nuts. After they had finished, two beautiful white beds were prepared, and when Hansel and Gretel lay down they felt as if they had gone to heaven.

The old woman had appeared to be most friendly, but she was really an old witch who had built the little bread house in order to lure children in. When anyone came into her power she killed, cooked, and ate him. Now, witches have red eyes and cannot see far, but, like beasts, they have a keen sense of smell and know when human beings pass by. When Hansel and Gretel fell into her hands, she laughed and said jeeringly: "I've got them now; they won't escape me." Early in the morning, before the children were awake, she arose, and when she saw them both sleeping so peacefully, with their round rosy cheeks, she muttered: "That'll be a dainty bite." Then she seized Hansel with her bony hands and carried him into a stable, and barred the door on him; he might scream as much as he liked, it did no good. Then she went to Gretel, shook her till she awoke, and cried: "Get up, you lazy-bones; fetch water and cook something for your brother. When he's fat I'll eat him up." Gretel began to cry bitterly, but it was no use; she had to do what the wicked witch bade her.

So the best food was cooked for poor Hansel, but Gretel got nothing but crab-shells. Every morning the old woman hobbled to

the stable and cried: "Hansel, put out your finger, that I may feel if you are getting fat." But Hansel always stretched out a bone, and the old dame, whose eyes were dim, couldn't see it and, thinking it was Hansel's finger, wondered why he fattened so slowly. When four weeks passed and Hansel remained thin, she decided to wait no longer. "Hi! Gretel," she called, "be quick and get some water. Hansel may be fat or thin, I'm going to kill him tomorrow and cook him." Oh! how the poor sister sobbed as she carried the water, and how the tears rolled down her cheeks! "Kind Heaven help us now!" she cried, "if only the wild beasts in the wood had eaten us, then at least we should have died together." "Just hold your peace," said the old hag, "it won't help you."

Early in the morning Gretel had to go and hang up the kettle full of water and light the fire. "First we'll bake," said the old dame, "I've heated the oven and kneaded the dough." She pushed

Gretel out to the oven, from which fiery flames were already issuing. "Creep in," said the witch, "and see if it's properly heated, so that we can shove in the bread." When Gretel got in she meant to close the oven and let the girl bake, that she might eat her up too. But Gretel perceived her intention and spoke: "I don't know how to do it; how do I get in?" "You silly goose!" said the hag, "the opening is big enough; see, I could get in myself;" and she poked her head into the oven. Then Gretel gave her a shove that sent her right in, shut the iron door, and drew the bolt. Gracious! how she yelled! it was horrible; but Gretel fled, and the wretched old woman was left to perish.

Gretel flew straight to Hansel, opened the stable door, and cried: "Hansel, we are free; the old witch is dead." Then Hansel sprang out, they rejoiced, and fell on each other's necks, and jumped for joy! And as they had no longer any cause for fear, they

went into the old hag's house, and there they found boxes with pearls and precious stones. "These are even better than pebbles," said Hansel, and crammed his pockets full; and Gretel said, "I, too, will bring some home;" and she filled her apron full. "But now," said Hansel, "let's go and get away from the witch's woods." When they had wandered for some hours they came to a big lake. "We can't get over," said Hansel, "I see no bridge of any kind." "Yes, and no ferryboat either," answered Gretel, "but look, there swims a white duck;" and she called out:

> *"Here are two children, mournful very,*
> *Seeing neither bridge nor ferry;*
> *Take us upon your white back,*
> *And row us over, quack, quack!"*

The duck swam toward them, and Hansel got on her back and bade his little sister sit beside him. "No," answered Gretel, "we should be too heavy for the duck; she shall carry us across separately." The good bird did this, and when they were safely on the other side and had gone on for a while, the wood became more familiar to them, and at length they saw their father's house in the distance. Then they started to run and, bounding into the house, fell on their father's neck. The man had not passed a happy hour since he left them in the woods, but the woman had died. Gretel shook out her apron so that the pearls and precious stones rolled about the room, and Hansel threw down one handful after the other out of his pocket. Thus all their troubles were ended, and they lived happily ever afterward.

Rumpelstiltzkin, or The Miller's Daughter

UNITED KINGDOM

There was once upon a time a poor miller who had a very beautiful daughter. Now, it happened one day that he had an audience with the King, and in order to appear a person of some importance he told him that he had a daughter who could spin straw into gold. "Now that's a talent worth having," said the King to the miller. "If your daughter is as clever as you say, bring her to my palace tomorrow and I'll put her to the test." When the girl was brought to him, he led her into a room full of straw, gave her a spinning-wheel and spindle, and said: "Now set to work and spin all night till dawn, and if by that time you haven't spun the straw into gold you shall die." Then he closed the door behind him and left her alone inside.

So the poor miller's daughter sat down and didn't know what in the world she was to do. She hadn't the least idea of how to spin straw into gold, and became at last so miserable that she began to cry. Suddenly the door opened and in stepped a tiny little man who said: "Good-evening, Miss Miller-maid. Why are you crying so bitterly?" "Oh!" answered the girl, "I have to spin straw into gold and haven't a notion how it's done." "What will you give me if I spin it for you?" asked the manikin. "My necklace," replied the girl. The little man took the necklace, sat himself down at the wheel, and whir! whir! whir! the wheel went round three times and the bobbin was full. Then he put on another, and whir! whir! whir! the wheel went round three times, and the second, too, was full; and so it went on till the morning, when all the straw was spun away and all the bobbins were full of gold.

As soon as the sun rose the King came, and when he perceived the gold he was astonished and delighted, but his heart only lusted more than ever after the precious metal. He had the miller's daughter put into another room full of straw, much bigger than the first, and bade her, if she valued her life, spin it all into gold before the following morning. The girl didn't know what to do and began to cry; then the door opened as before, and the tiny little man appeared and said: "What'll you give me if I spin the straw into gold for you?" "The ring from my finger," answered the girl. The manikin took the ring, and whir! round went the spinning-wheel again, and when morning broke he had spun all the straw into glittering gold. The King was pleased beyond measure at the sight, but his greed for gold was still not satisfied, and he had the miller's daughter brought into a yet bigger room full of straw, and he said: "You must spin all this away in the night; but if you succeed this time you shall become my wife." "She's only a miller's daughter, it's true," he thought, "but I couldn't find a richer wife if I were to search the whole world over." When the girl was alone the little man appeared for the third time and said: "What'll you give me if I spin the straw for you once again?" "I've nothing more to give," answered the girl. "Then promise me when you are queen to give me your first child." "Who knows what will happen before

that?" thought the miller's daughter; and besides, she saw no other way out of it, so she promised the manikin what he demanded, and he set to work once more and spun the straw into gold. When the King came in the morning and found everything as he had desired, he straightway made her his wife, and the miller's daughter became a queen.

When a year had passed a beautiful son was born to her, and she thought no more of the little man, till all of a sudden one day he stepped into her room and said: "Now give me what you promised." The Queen was in a great state, and offered the little man all the riches in her kingdom if he would only leave her the child. But the manikin said: "No, a living creature is dearer to me than all the treasure in the world." Then the Queen began to cry and sob so bitterly that the little man felt sorry for her and said: "I'll give you three days to guess my name, and if you find it out in that time you may keep your child."

Then the Queen pondered the whole night over all the names she had ever heard, and sent a messenger to scour the land and to pick up far and near any names he should come across. When the little man arrived on the following day she began with Kasper, Melchior, Belshazzar, and all the other names she knew, in a string, but at each one the manikin called out: "That's not my name." The next day she sent to inquire the names of all the people in the neighborhood, and had a long list of the most uncommon and extraordinary for the little man when he made his appearance. "Is your name, perhaps, Sheepshanks, Crookshanks, Spindleshanks?" but he always replied: "That's not my name." On the third day the messenger returned and announced: "I have not been able to find any new names, but as I came upon a high hill round the corner of the wood, where the foxes and hares bid each other good-night, I saw a little house, and in front of the house burned a fire, and round the fire sprang the most grotesque little man, hopping on one leg and crying:

'*Tomorrow I brew, today I bake,*
And then the child away I'll take;
For little deems my royal dame
That Rumpelstiltzkin is my name!'"

You may imagine the Queen's delight at hearing the name, and when the little man stepped in shortly afterward and asked: "Now, my lady queen, what's my name?" she asked first: "Is your name Conrad?" "No." "Is your name Harry?" "No." "Is your name, perhaps, Rumpelstiltzkin?" "Some demon has told you that! Some demon has told you that!" screamed the little man, and in his rage drove his right foot so far into the ground that it sank in up to his waist; then in a passion he seized the left foot with both hands and tore himself in two.

Yael and Mulwarra

AUSTRALIA

Once upon a time there was a bird spirit named Yael who spent his time roaming the far reaches of the heavens. He wore a long golden cloak of feathers that flowed out behind his back and up over his head to form a mask around where his eyes would be. However, while Yael's body was human, he had no face. Inside his mask was nothing but endless blue sky, and though he had legs, he never used them because his golden cloak would take him anywhere he wished to go.

Yarnu, Yael's father, was anxious for his son to settle down with one of the many female spirits who lived in the heavens. But Yael would not. Try as Yarnu might to persuade his son, Yael would not marry. Yarnu was sad, for as far as he knew he was the only bird spirit without grandchildren.

One day, as Yael floated gently above the Earth, he thought of the awful plight of being human. He could think of nothing worse than being a clumsy human tied to the Earth by gravity. As he floated he noticed a young girl walking along a cliff edge near the ocean. Her long legs carried her softly. "How strange," he said to himself. "She's quite graceful for a human." He floated along above her and marveled at her quiet step, for humans were usually awkward, lumbering creatures who had no respect for the Earth.

Yet this girl walked carefully, as though she could not take in enough of the rugged beauty around her.

The girl must have sensed Yael's presence because suddenly she looked upward and at the very same time she tripped over a rock and plunged headlong over the cliff, down toward the sharp rocks below.

Yael quickly swooped down to catch the girl and then flew back up into the heavens with her in his arms. When she opened her eyes and saw her rescuer's empty face, she gasped in fear.

"Where am I?" she whispered. "Who are you? Am I dead?"

"No," Yael laughed. "You're still very much alive. I saved you from your fall off the cliff. I am a bird spirit."

"A bird spirit," she said wonderingly. Though she'd heard of such things, never before had she seen one.

"Thank you, bird spirit, for saving me. My name is Mulwarra and I am a human."

"Yes, I know," he replied. "I am Yael."

Yael and Mulwarra flew around in the sky and Yael showed her how beautiful the Earth could be from above.

"It's wonderful," she sighed. "So vibrant and glorious."

Mulwarra's enthusiasm made Yael want to show her even more of the glory of the heavens. "Would you like to see something else?" he asked.

When Mulwarra nodded, he curved around in the sky and soon they were soaring far, far away. As they explored the stars and planets they found a mutual love of nature and the world — of beauty and freedom.

After some time Mulwarra asked, "Yael, why did you save me?"

Yael pondered this question for some time. Indeed, there was no simple answer. Something about this girl had touched him, and now this impulse had turned into something even deeper. He decided to take Mulwarra to meet his father, Yarnu.

When Yael appeared before Yarnu with Mulwarra in his arms, Yarnu was not pleased. "What's that thing you have in your arms?" he asked.

"I am a human," Mulwarra said bravely.

"So you are, you poor clumsy thing," replied Yarnu pityingly. "But why have you brought this thing of Earth here?" he asked, turning to Yael.

Yael hesitated to speak of what was now clearly in his heart. Instead he replied, "She fell from a cliff and I could not let her die."

Yarnu looked closely at Yael. Surely his glorious son had not fallen in love with this pathetic girl? Immediately he decided that

Mulwarra must be disposed of. Yarnu cringed at the thought of fat, clumsy grandchildren.

"Son, why don't you put the heavy one down and rest?" he suggested softly.

But Yael refused. He knew his father well enough to know this was a trick. If he let Mulwarra go, he knew her weight would immediately send her plummeting back down to Earth.

"You cannot carry her day and night," Yarnu said crossly. "Why not share her weight with the others?"

Yael would not agree to this either. He knew of his father's influence. One word from him and the other bird spirits would drop her.

"Ach! Then go away!" said Yarnu disgustedly, once he realized his tricks would not work.

And so Yael flew off with Mulwarra and showed her other heavenly wonders. Though he was disappointed in his father, he had hoped that he would soon understand.

Much time passed as Yael and Mulwarra continued to wander the skies. They returned only now and then to see Yarnu. Yarnu waited patiently for his son to tire of the Earth girl, but his wait was in vain. Mulwarra, too, began to fall in love with Yael. When Yarnu saw how she looked at his son, he was filled with rage.

One day, Mulwarra said to Yael, "I love your world, Yael. It's very beautiful, but very different from mine."

"What is wrong?" asked Yael as he looked at her sad face.

"Oh, Yael," she said. "I love you, but I miss the feel of the earth beneath my feet. I want to see the flowers and the birds and the trees. I miss my family. And … I wish you had a face. I want to be able to see you frown and be happy or sad."

"I would like to please you," he sighed. "But I am a bird spirit, and not a man."

Yarnu chuckled happily. "At last! The boy is coming to his senses," he told himself. "Soon he will throw that clumsy creature away." When Yael visited his father next, Yarnu welcomed him warmly.

"Come to your senses, have you?" he asked eagerly, ignoring Mulwarra.

"I believe I have," replied Yael.

"Wonderful, wonderful," said Yarnu happily. "Well, drop her off gently my boy. When you return I will have some beautiful spirits waiting for you."

"I'm afraid you don't understand, Father," said Yael. "I do not want to let Mulwarra go. I want to give up my spirit form and become human. I know you have the power to help me do it."

Yarnu was furious. He flew around the sky in a snarling rage, sending sparks leaping around him. Then he swooped down and tried to knock Mulwarra from Yael's arms. Finally he screeched, "Leave, both of you!" and flew off into furthest heaven.

Yael and Mulwarra grew sadder and sadder. It seemed there would be no human form for Yael. They no longer roamed the heavens, but sat in silence, holding each other gently.

"Hmph," complained Yarnu, when he finally returned, "he might as well be human for all the flying he does now."

Now, though Yarnu had many faults, he loved his son deeply. Though he was a very strong-willed, temperamental old spirit, in the end he wanted only what was best for his son. He called Yael to him.

"Son, if you give up this human, I will give you anything you wish for," he offered. But Yael only shook his head.

"Alas, I know when I am beaten," the old spirit said sadly. "I will grant your request. But you know that once you leave this heavenly kingdom you can never return?"

"Yes, Father."

"And you understand that though I may give you a human face and form, I cannot make the human people accept you as you may want. You will never be completely one of them."

Yael accepted this.

Yarnu spread out his feather cloak and began to glow a deep, dark red, a red that was of the Mother Earth. The glow spread away from the old spirit and over Yael and Mulwarra, completely enveloping them in its dark mist. Yael felt himself growing heavier and heavier. Then, suddenly, both he and Mulwarra were falling down, down, down through the heavens, past the sun and planets and back to Earth. The ground rushed up to meet them, but just before they collided, their fall was halted and they landed gently in the sand.

Once they'd recovered their breath, Mulwarra turned to look eagerly at Yael. "Oh, Yael!" she cried happily. "You look wonderful! You are so handsome. Now let me show you the delights of my world!"

Yael smiled happily and hand in hand they stood up. But when Yael tried to walk he fell over. "How do you move these things?" he asked, as he felt his muscly legs.

"But you've always had legs," she answered, laughing.

"Yes, I've always had them, but I've never felt their weight and I've never walked in my life."

"It's simple," she said kindly. "You simply stand up and put one foot in front of the other. You'll soon get used to it."

Yael stood up, took two steps and fell over once again. They continued in this way all along the beach. He did learn, eventually, but he was never able to walk as naturally as Mulwarra. He was always a bit wobbly and had difficulty walking in a straight line.

When Mulwarra returned to her home, her family was overjoyed to have her back. They hugged and kissed her and asked her where she'd been. When she told them her strange tale, they didn't believe her, but patted her on the head nicely, thinking she'd been in the sun too long.

"And who is this stranger?" they asked as they looked at Yael.

"This is Yael," Mulwarra replied, "The bird spirit I was telling you about. Only he is human now and he has come to live with us."

Mulwarra's family looked nervously at Yael. But it was obvious that the two were in love, so they held out their hands in welcome. As Yael went to take their hands, he tripped and fell over, pulling Mulwarra's mother with him.

"He's still a bit wobbly," explained Mulwarra, as she helped them both up.

Mulwarra's family tried to like Yael, but they were puzzled by his strange behavior. He didn't eat red meat, but only seeds and raw worms. He'd been taken on several hunts but always ruined things by falling over. One night they'd cooked him a special meal of brush turkey and he only cried and cried. Instead of eating it, he'd gone and buried it. Indeed, it did not matter what bird they chose to eat, Yael always wept uncontrollably when he saw the dead body.

The elders grew more and more worried at Yael's strange behavior. They held a special meeting to try to understand why Mulwarra's friend was so odd.

Yael's father recounted the strange story his daughter had told him upon her return. The old men were angry they hadn't been informed earlier. Spirits could be very bad trouble and they didn't want any trouble.

"He could be an evil spirit in disguise," said one.

"Waiting for the right moment to bring us harm," said another.

"He seems harmless, though," said Mulwarra's father. "He's just not like the rest of us."

"Not like the rest of us?" they repeated crossly. "That proves we're right," said the old men. "There's no place for evil spirits here. You must get rid of him before he causes any more trouble."

Mulwarra's father took pity on the young lovers and warned them that it was no longer safe for them to stay. He gave them plenty of food and a good sharp spear, and sent them off to find a place where they could live happily.

For many days they followed the line of the cliff edge. Wherever they went, though, people would always notice Yael's wobbly legs. When they spoke to him they grew frightened of the strange stories he told. How could a man know so much about the heavens they reasoned, unless he was an evil spirit fallen from the sky? And so the trouble would begin once again.

One day, as they were sitting on the warm sand, bathing their tired feet in the ocean, Yael said, "I was stupid to think I could be a human. Your people will never accept me, no matter where we go."

Mulwarra sighed. "And yours will not accept me either," she said.

Now Yarnu had been watching his son's life grow more and more difficult. He'd been reluctantly impressed by Mulwarra's devotion to his son and the fact that never once did she criticize him. Though he knew he could never return Yael to spirit form, there was one thing he could do. And he hoped it would work because it was their last chance at happiness.

Yarnu began to glow. But this time he glowed blue, not red. Yael and Mulwarra sensed his presence and looked up to see the luminous, blue glow in the sky.

"It's your father," said Mulwarra.

"I wonder what he's up to," replied Yael, puzzled.

The vibrant blue glow floated out of Yarnu and down to the young couple below. They were bathed in the calm, gentle light and slowly began to feel a languid flowing freedom wash over them. The ocean waves slowly overtook them; they watched in surprise as their toes disappeared, then their feet, then their legs. Soon they were both part of the sea and yet still their individual selves.

"This is wonderful!" gurgled Mulwarra, as she surfed through the waves.

"I love it!" cried Yael. "I feel light again." And over and over they rolled, frolicking and giggling like young seals.

"Thank you, Father!" they both called as he followed them out to the sea.

"Be happy, my two sea spirits," he returned. "I will visit you again when my first grandchild is born."

Then Yarnu flew off, muttering to himself, "At least now my grandchildren will not be so clumsy." He smiled contentedly, but you couldn't see, of course, because his face went on forever. Just like the endless blue sea.

The Frog Prince

There was once a handsome young Prince who had the misfortune to offend a Wicked Fairy. To avenge herself she turned him into a frog, and put him in a well.

It happened that the well was in the courtyard of a Palace, and on the fine days, when the sun shone warmly, the King's youngest daughter came there to amuse herself by throwing a Golden Ball into the air and catching it as it fell. The poor Frog Prince watched her and thought she was the prettiest Princess he had ever seen.

One day the Princess missed the Golden Ball, and it bounced and fell into the water. She ran to the edge of the well and gazed down; but the Golden Ball had sunk far out of sight. She began to cry bitterly.

The Frog Prince popped his head out of the water.

"Don't cry, Princess!" he said. "What will you give me if I bring your ball from the bottom of the well?"

"Oh," replied the Princess. "My pretty frock, my diamonds—even the crown on my head. Only bring my ball back to me!"

"I do not want your frock or your diamonds or your crown," said the Frog Prince. "But if you will promise to let me eat off of your plate, and drink out of your cup, and sleep in your silken bed—I will bring your ball back to you."

And the Princess promised. For she said to herself: "What a silly frog! He will never find me."

The Frog Prince dived to the bottom of the well, and presently came up with the Golden Ball in his mouth.

The Princess had no sooner snatched it from him than she forgot all about her promise, and ran back to the Palace laughing with joy.

The next day, as she sat at dinner with the King and his Courtiers, there was a gentle knock at the door.

Then the Princess dropped her spoon with a clatter on her plate, for she knew that it was the frog come to claim her promise. She ran to the door and opened it, and, behold! there was the frog, whom she had quite forgotten; she was sadly frightened, and, shutting the door as fast as she could, returned to her seat.

"What is the matter, daughter?" asked the King. "There is someone knocking at the door, and your rosy cheeks are quite pale."

Then the Princess had to tell her father all that had happened the day before—and of all the promises she had given. The King frowned and said: "People who make promises must honor them. Open the door, and let the frog in."

The Princess opened the door and the Frog Prince hopped into the room.

"Lift me up beside you," he cried, "that I may eat off of your plate, and drink out of your cup." The Princess did as he asked her, and was obliged to finish her dinner with the frog beside her. When they had finished, the Frog Prince hopped down from his chair and cried: "I have had enough to eat, and now I am tired. Take me up and lay me on your silken pillow, that I may go to sleep."

Then the Princess began to cry. It was dreadful to think that an ugly frog, all cold and damp from the well, should sleep in her pretty white bed. But her father frowned again and said: "People who make promises must honor them. He gave you back your Golden Ball and you must do as he asks."

The Princess did so; and as soon as it was light the frog jumped up, hopped down stairs, and went out of the house.

"Now," thought the Princess, "he is gone, and I shall be troubled with him no more."

But she was mistaken; for, when night came again, she heard the same tapping at the door, and, when she opened it, the frog came in and remained as before; and the third night he did the same; but, when the Princess awoke on the following morning, she was astonished to see, instead of the frog, a handsome prince gazing on her with the most beautiful eyes that ever were seen!

He then told her that he had been enchanted by a fairy who had changed him into a frog, and so he was doomed to remain till a Princess should let him live with her for three days. "You," said the Prince, "have broken this cruel charm, and now I have nothing to wish for but that you should go with me into my father's kingdom, where I will marry you, and love you as long as you live."

The young Princess was not slow in consenting; and, as they spoke, a gay coach drove up with eight beautiful horses, and behind rode the Prince's faithful servant, who had long bewailed the misfortunes of his dear master. Then all set out full of joy for the Prince's kingdom; which they reached safely, and lived happily there for many years.

The Beginning of Narran Lake

AUSTRALIA

Old Baiame said to his two young wives, Birra-nulu and Kunnan-beili, "I have stuck a white feather between the hind legs of a bee, and am going to let it go and then follow it to its nest, that I may get honey. While I go for the honey, you two go out and get frogs and yams, then meet me at Coorigil Spring, where we will camp, for sweet and clear is the water there."

The wives, taking their goolays, or net bags, and yam sticks, went out as he told them. Having gone far, and dug out many yams and frogs, they were tired when they reached Coorigil, and seeing the cool, fresh water, they longed to bathe. But first they built a bough shade, and there left the goolays holding their food, and the yams and frogs they had found.

When their camp was ready for the coming of Baiame (who, having wooed his wives with a nulla-nulla, kept them obedient by fear of the same weapon), the wives went to the spring to bathe. Gladly they plunged in, having first divested themselves of their goomillas, or string belts, which they were still young enough to wear, and which they left on the ground near the spring.

Scarcely were they enjoying the cool rest the water gave their hot, tired limbs, when they were seized and swallowed by two Kurrias, or crocodiles.

Having swallowed the wives, the Kurrias dived into an opening in the side of the spring, which was the entrance to an underground watercourse leading to the Narran River. Through this passage they went, taking all the water from the spring with them into the Narran, whose course they also dried as they went along.

Meantime, Baiame, unaware of the fate of his wives, was honey hunting. He had followed the bee with the white feather on it for some distance; then the bee flew on to some boodha, or saltbush flowers, and would move no farther.

Baiame said, "Something has happened, or the bee would not stay here and refuse to be moved on toward its nest. I must go to Coorigil Spring and see if my wives are safe. Something terrible has surely happened."

And Baiame turned in haste toward the spring.

When he reached there he saw the bough shed his wives had made, he saw the yams they had dug from the ground, and he saw the frogs, but Birra-nulu and Kunnan-beili he saw not.

He called aloud for them. But no answer. He went toward the spring; on the edge of it he saw the goomillas of his wives. He looked into the spring and, seeing it dry, he said, "It is the work of the Kurrias; they have opened the underground passage and gone with my wives to the river, and opening the passage has dried the spring. Well do I know where the passage joins the Narran, and there will I swiftly go."

Arming himself with spears and woggaras, he started in pursuit.

He soon reached the deep hole where the underground channel of the Coorigil joined the Narran. There he saw what he had never seen before, namely, this deep hole gone dry. And he

said, "They have emptied the holes as they went along, taking the water with them. But well know I the deep holes of the river. I will not follow the bend, thus trebling the distance I have to go, but I will cut across from big hole to big hole, and by so doing I may yet get ahead of the Kurrias."

Swiftly on sped Baiame, making short cuts from big hole to big hole, and his track is still marked by the morillas, or pebbly ridges, that stretch down the Narran, pointing in toward the deep holes.

Every hole as he came to it he found dry, until at last he reached the end of the Narran; the hole there was still quite wet and muddy. Then he knew he was near his enemies, and soon he saw them.

He managed to get, unseen, a little way ahead of the Kurrias. He hid himself behind a big dheal tree. As the Kurrias came near they separated, each turning to go in a different direction. Quickly Baiame hurled one spear after another, wounding both Kurrias, who writhed with pain and lashed their tails furiously, making great hollows in the ground, which the water they had brought with them quickly filled. Thinking they might again escape him, Baiame drove them from the water with his spears, and then, at close quarters, he killed them with his woggaras.

And ever afterwards, at floodtime, the Narran flowed into this hollow which the Kurrias in their writhings had made.

When Baiame saw that the Kurrias were quite dead, he cut them open and took out the bodies of his wives. They were covered with wet slime and seemed quite lifeless, but he carried them and laid them on two nests of red ants. Then he sat down at some little distance and watched them. The ants quickly covered the bodies, cleaned them rapidly of the wet slime, and soon Baiame noticed the muscles of the wives twitching.

"Ah," he said, "there is life; they feel the sting of the ants."

Almost as he spoke came a sound as a thunderclap, but the sound seemed to come from the ears of the wives. And as the echo was dying away, slowly the wives rose to their feet. For a moment they stood apart, a dazed expression on their faces. Then they clung together, shaking as if stricken with a deadly fear. But Baiame came to them and explained how they had been rescued from the Kurrias by him. He bade them to beware of ever bathing in the deep holes of the Narran, lest such holes be the haunt of Kurrias.

Then he bade them look at the water now at Boogira, and said, "Soon the black swans will find their way here, the pelicans and the ducks; where there was dry land and stones in the past, in the future there will be water and waterfowl. From henceforth, when the Narran runs it will run into this hole, and by the spreading of its waters a big lake will be made."

And what Baiame said has come to pass, as the Narran Lake shows, with its large sheet of water, spreading for miles, the home of thousands of wildfowl.

The Voyage of Sinbad the Sailor

ARABIA

A story is carried from Baghdad—though who can tell if it is true?—of a young man called Sinbad the Porter. Sinbad was known at all the local inns for his beautiful singing voice, and he would often sing in return for a coin or a bite to eat. He was summoned one day to a great house built of white and wine-colored marble on the outskirts of the city. An old man was sitting on the vine-covered terrace and asked him to sing, which he willingly did:

> *Oh I have carried golden treasure*
> *Half across Arabia's lands,*
> *And I have seen the cost of pleasure*
> *Pouring out of rich men's hands.*
> *But do not think of me as rich, sir,*
> *Because I carry treasure chests,*
> *For I count myself much richer*
> *When I lay them down and rest.*

I am just a poor young porter—
All my meat is caught from rivers,
All the wines I drink are water—
All I carry, I deliver.

The song pleased the old man, and he took a great liking to the porter.

"The pleasure a good song gives can't be paid for with money alone," said the old man. "Let me give you something of mine. I shall give you the story of my life, which is moderately interesting. My name is Sinbad too. But I am Sinbad the Sailor."

I was born the son of a rich father who died and left me a lot of money. Being a particularly clever boy, I made the sensible decision to invest the money. I invested it in drink and expensive food and stylish clothes and in buying myself a lot of friends at the local inn. Before long I found that my investment had left me with hardly a penny. To tell you the truth, I did not want to be poor in my old age.

So I sold everything I owned and bought instead a silk-sailed ship and cargo. I employed a captain, and we set sail for the rest of the world, turning a furrow through the sea as straight and certain as an arrow through a blue sky. I was confident of making my fortune as a merchant.

One day a solitary island came into view from the mast top: two or three trees and a smooth, gray beach the color of the atolls in the great Western Ocean.

Some of the sailors were tired of the blood swilling in their veins with the motion of the ship, and we took it into our heads to draw alongside the island and walk about on dry land. The captain was sleeping below-decks. We did not trouble to wake

him because all we wanted were a friendly fire, a baked fish, and a short walk. Then we would be ready to set off again. Two of the men even brought a laundry barrel from the ship to do their washing in.

Ali lit a fire, and I made a tour of the island, but there was not a lot to recommend it. We were just deciding that no one could live there, without fresh water, when suddenly Abdul caught sight of a fountain—a geyser, rather—at a great distance from us. Its water gushed higher and higher, seemingly to the height of a castle tower, then dropped out of sight.

"I have been aboard ship for too long, the ground still seems to be moving," I said, embarrassed by losing my balance and falling over. Then the captain's voice drifted to us on the wind.

"Aboard! Aboard! Or you are all dead men!"

"The island is sinking!" someone cried.

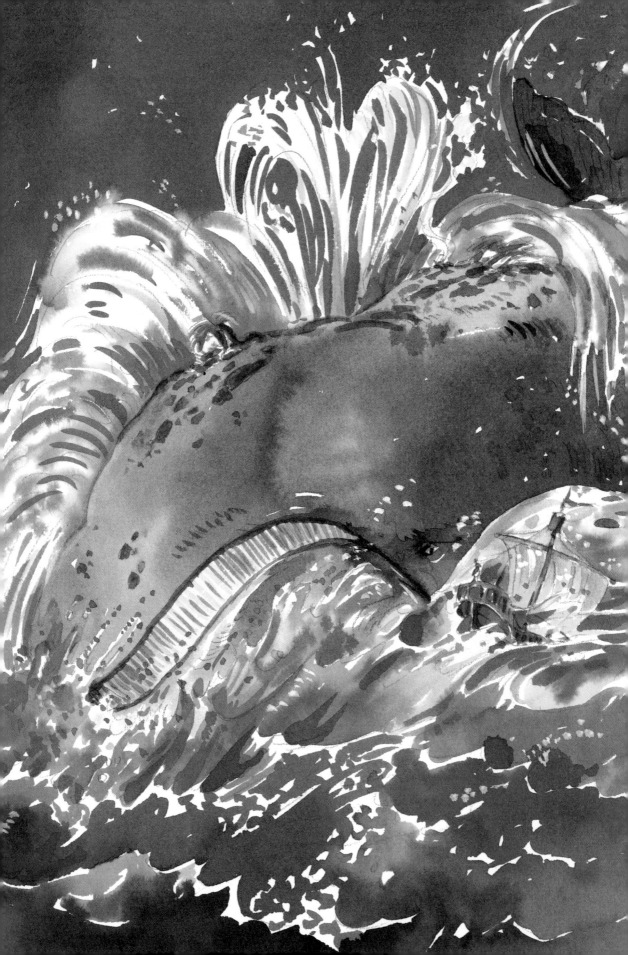

"The island is moving!" shouted another.

A deep roaring beneath us was followed by a second eruption of water from the geyser. It spouted so high that the spray reached us on the wind and soaked us to the skin in a second.

Amidst the spray, I could see the captain giving orders for the ship to pull away. The space of water increased between our landing party and the vessel. Some men ran to the water and leapt in. Others shouted at the captain, calling him names or begging him to pull ashore again. Only one or two of his words reached us across the opening gap.

"Whale!...Fire has woken the whale...."

Well may you hold your head in wonder, friend. We had indeed moored alongside a giant whale, and the fire we had lit on its back had disturbed it out of a sleep centuries long. The sandy silt of the ocean had washed over the whale, and the winds had brought seeds and spores and planted its sparse vegetation. But as it rolled in pain, our fire beginning to burn through its hide (and making an awful stench), the shallow-rooted trees were washed away like toothpicks, and the sand swirled round our knees as we stumbled to and fro. The whale dived.

One sailor was thrown high out of the water by the massive tail—believe me, friend, those tail-flukes were larger than galleon sails—and the tail fell on us like the greatest tree in all the gum forests of Arabia.

To the end of my days, I shall weary Allah with my thanks. The barrel full of my fellow sailors' washing rolled toward me across the water. I pulled myself across it and floated away, while my sailor friends swam down with the whale to the kingdom where only the fish can breathe. Friend, friend, it makes me sweat saltwater just to think about it.

The ship had long since gone. I was alone on the ocean with the smell of scorched whale in my nostrils. I began to paddle with my feet, and my lonely voyage, as you can imagine, was so long and tiring that I do not remember reaching land.

I woke up beside my barrel on a white beach to find, to my great surprise, that I was alive. I also found that the fish had eaten many holes in my feet, and only with pain and difficulty did I climb the beach and explore.

I saw no one, friend, and nothing. Under the trees the undergrowth was thick: a perfect home for wild animals. Why else did I climb that tree? But from the topmost branches I could see a long, long way.

I saw no one, friend, and nothing. In another direction, however, I glimpsed a shining white dome. Surely it was a fine mosque at the heart of a splendid city. Its white curve seemed so massive that I was almost afraid to approach.

When I finally reached it, I walked around it five times before I gave up hope of finding a door. Its whiteness was dazzling in the sun. I tried to climb up it, but the white surface was so polished and smooth that I slithered down to the ground again every time. I exhausted myself in the midday heat, and that is why I was sitting on the ground in the shade of the white dome when the sun went dark.

I have seen tropical suns set like a single clap of hands. I have seen the moon forget its rightful place and push in front of the sun. But this was no eclipse or sunset.

Looking up, I saw that the sun had been blotted out by the shape of a gigantic bird. Its claws were as large as the tusks of elephants, one toe the thickness of a tree trunk. Its wings were as huge as my terror, and its feathers as black as my miserable fate. For now I realized that the white dome I was sitting under was nothing other than the bird's unhatched egg. And as slowly and certainly as a ship on a whirlpool is sucked circling down, the huge bird was wheeling down toward me.

From the well of my memory, I drew up the strange and wonderful tales I had heard at Baghdad harbor. I recalled travelers' descriptions of the Giant Rukh, a bird whose wingspan half covered the sky. I undoubtedly was squatting in the shadow of just such a bird, and my only hope of life lay in staying hidden under the egg.

A vast, stinking warmth enveloped me as the rukh settled over her egg, and I found myself somewhere between the clawed feet, a pouch of bird down pressing on my head with all the weight of a feather bed. It pushed off my turban, which unwound at my feet. That was when I formed my plan of escape. Lying down alongside one horny talon—as thick and rough as a log—I tied myself securely to the rukh's claw, using the cloth of my turban. Then I went to sleep to escape the pains of fear in my heart and the pains of hunger in my stomach.

I woke up in time only to wish that I had stayed asleep. The rukh had risen off its egg and was climbing a furlong with every beat of its wings. The egg below soon looked no bigger than a white bean; the whole island soon looked no bigger than a pea.

I wished to commend my life's good deeds to Allah so that He might be merciful to me, but I could remember lamentably few. So I vowed to behave much better if Allah, in His mercy, would grant me the opportunity. Still the bird soared higher until I thought it must roost among the beams of the sun. The air was so thin that my lungs shriveled to the size of walnuts and blood abandoned my head. I regained consciousness just as the rukh swooped down below the rim of a black canyon and glided down into a valley.

"Oh, Allah is truly merciful!" I cried. "He saved me from the gulf of the ocean and from the vault of the sky and has set my feet on solid ground again." Fumbling at the knots of cloth, I rolled away from under the rukh and bundled together my turban.

"Oh, Allah is full of subtlety," I shrieked. "Was a drowning too good for Sinbad or starvation too merciful? Was it not bad enough to be eaten by the rukh? Was Fate preserving me for this miserable pit?"

For everywhere I looked were bare black rocks, and the sides of the canyon were sheer. Between every rock and strangling every boulder, huge black serpents coiled and writhed about. The rukh that had brought me to this pit of despair stretched out its grotesque head and snatched up a serpent as though it were a wriggling worm. Then with a scrabbling of gravel it ran forward and took off, spiraling up to the narrow blue slit of sky a mile above me. It scarcely interested me, but indeed it was not gravel that the rukh scuffed up. Everywhere, but everywhere, the ground was sprinkled with precious stones—diamonds, emeralds, sapphires, and rubies—more treasure than even the greed of a young Sinbad had ever imagined. And shall I tell you, friend, my only thoughts at seeing this undreamt-of wealth? I wept because the diamonds hurt my feet to tread on.

Those hideous land-serpents rippled as hugely and shined as blackly and were as many as the swelling waves on a night sea. The roots of my soul shriveled, and I fell on my face, waiting to be swallowed, strangled, or poisoned by their licking fangs.

Just then–I tell no lies, but believe me if you can—a slab of raw meat fell on my head.

"A serpent is crawling over me," I thought, praying for a quick death. But as the juices trickled through my hair, I decided I was in fact wearing a side of mutton. Perhaps it was a hint from Allah that I should eat heartily before I was eaten, so I crawled out from under the meat only to be narrowly missed by another side of mutton, bouncing down the canyon wall.

Have you heard the rumor, friend, of a place called the Valley of Diamonds? Well, I can vouch that the place exists. There are indeed merchants who grow rich on the diamonds, but they do not—they dare not—climb down among the snakes. Instead, they pitch slabs of raw meat into the ravine. The diamonds and so forth become embedded in the meat, then the giant rukhs, hunting for food, fly down and carry the mutton out of the ravine. Let my story tell you what happens next.

When I realized what was happening, I gathered up as many jewels as my pocket would hold, crawled back under the slab of mutton and clung on to it as mortal man clings to life.

A rukh came hunting for food to feed its chick.

I and my meat were lifted off the ground in the grip of its giant claws, and soon the serpents in the valley looked no bigger than bloodworms in a barrel. The bird carried its food to a nest in the crook of a mountain ledge. It immediately began tearing at the meat with its gruesome beak and pushing pieces into the pink gullet of its chick, a creature as big as a cow.

One peck slashed open my chest, the next would certainly rip out my heart.

"Oh, Allah!" I cried. "Did my mother's care and my father's money make me fit for nothing but to be breakfast to a baby rukh?"

Just at that moment, an avalanche of rocks tumbled past the ledge, and a great din of shouts and hoots up above frightened the rukh off its nest. One solitary merchant lowered himself on a rope to the ledge and began prodding the meat.

"There are no jewels there, my good fellow," I said.

At the sound of my voice, the merchant leapt backward. At the sight of me crawling from under the meat, he fell on his knees and began praying. I suppose I was *not* as clean as on the day my mother bore me: caked in sea salt and bird-lime, and red from head to foot with meat juices and blood.

"Forgive me, friend," I said, "for I know that cleanliness is close to Allah's heart. But if you would be so good as to help me off this unpleasant ledge, I would willingly share with you the treasure whose weight so discourteously prevents me getting to my feet." So saying, I fainted, quite overcome with hunger, weariness, and pain.

I received from the merchant the most precious of Allah's gifts: hospitality. He fed and cared for me, and only grudgingly accepted half my immense riches. He found me buyers for my diamonds, emeralds, sapphires, and rubies. And, when I was fully recovered, he directed me to a coastal harbor where my newfound wealth bought not just one ship but a whole fleet.

Unfortunately, not one captain among those who sailed in and out of the harbor had heard of Baghdad. Imagine it, friend! that some of the islands of the world have drifted on the winds and tides so far from the world's center that the inhabitants have never heard of Baghdad!

I sent the fleet in all directions, one following the Dog Star, one the Pole Star, one the Pleiades, and one the Red Planet, with instructions to trade at every port until they found knowledge of Baghdad. I myself boarded the ship with the richest cargo, opened the sails fully, and ran before any and every wind. For who sends the wind but Allah?

"Who sends the wind but Allah?" I crowed, sighting an island one morning.

But the captain said, "Some devil sent this one," and he bent his head on to the wheel and wrung his hands. He ordered the sails to be reefed in, and the ship turned to put the island behind us, but no sooner had we turned than a pirate ship rushed down on us. We lay between the ship and shore with not an inch of sail blowing.

The captain recognized both the island and the approaching ship, and he cursed his fate for bringing him to those waters. I begged him to tell us why he was lying full length, beating the deck with his fists. I begged him to tell us what to expect. But he only moaned pitifully and said, "Expect death, young man. Expect to die!"

The pirate ship was manned by a crew of dwarfs, wizened, yellow little men. They stood no higher than my thigh, but they

bit and scratched and leapt on us from the rigging where whole hoards of them swung about, shrieking and jabbering and baring their long yellow teeth.

Our clothes and skin in tatters, we huddled together at the stern, powerless to fight these darting, treacherous dwarfs with our slow fists and short, feeble cutlasses. They took control of the ship, let out all the sails, and steered us at full speed for the island. The island's true name, by the way, is the Isle of Zughb.

In the shallows, they carried us ashore, four or five dwarfs supporting each sailor. Then, as the last of us was thrown down on the sand, they all leapt aboard our ship and drew away from shore.

"Allah be praised," I said. "They may have been the most ugly creatures living, but at least they did not kill us, they were obviously thieves of mercy." O Sinbad, what kind of fool did your parents feed and educate? Did I sit on that beach and call those dwarfs thieves of mercy? They were no more merciful than one who puts cheese in the traps to feed poor hungry mice!

Behind the beach stood a towering fort surrounded by a high wall. Facing us was a gate worked all in ivory that stood half open, so we went inside and looked about.

We saw no one, friend, and nothing, but for a few cooking pots—as huge as horse troughs—some barbecue skewers longer than spears, and a few broken benches. Littering the deserted courtyard were several hundred white bones—put out for the owners' dogs, or so we assumed.

As no one answered our greetings, we curled up in our cloaks and slept, I, believing that my greatest misfortune lay in losing my cargo and ship. Fool that I was, fool that I was.

At sunset we were woken by the earth shaking under us. The ivory gates swung fully open, and a grotesque giant shuffled in and bolted them behind him. His head could only have pleased his mother: his cheeks hung down to his chest like a camel's dewlaps; he was as bald and tusked as a walrus; and the folds of skin under his eyes would have made hammocks for sailors; his ears draped over his shoulders and he barked a great deal, dragging his knuckles along the ground so that his nails, like two farm harrows, plowed up the soil.

The giant lit a fire, sat down beside it, and then looked us over thoughtfully. We were no surprise to him: the draws had simply made their regular delivery. A barricade of fat black fingers trapped me against a wall and rolled me into his black palm as though I were a sweetmeat. The giant poked and prodded me, but as I was still thin from my earlier shipwreck I did not please him. Instead he picked up the fat ship's cook between finger and thumb and cooked him on a spit over the fire, crunching him up with obvious satisfaction, and spitting out the larger bones.

Almost at once he fell asleep for the night, leaving us desperate with fear but unable to climb the high, smooth wall of the fort.

Every day was the same: the giant went out in the morning, bolted the gates, and came back in the evening with a ravenous appetite. He would choose the fattest sailor from the crew and roast and eat him barbecued for supper.

"O Allah, decider of all fates," we cried out, shivering with terror, "could you not have let the ship flounder or be swallowed by a whale? This is no way for a Believer or native of Baghdad to meet his end. We should have thrown ourselves into the sea when we first saw the pirate dwarfs." In short, it seemed time to act.

There were only a handful of us skinny sailors left. I suggested that the giant would soon start eating us two at a time. "In order to defend ourselves we must attack," I said. "But first we must know our escape route. Let's tie these benches together into a ladder and be ready to climb the wall tonight…."

That evening, after the ship's second lieutenant had satisfied the giant's hunger, we watched the ugly brute settle down to sleep and then we crept to the fireside. Hauling two of the skewers across the coals, we heated their points white-hot and, carrying them as undertakers carry coffins, we ran at the head of the sleeping cannibal. His snores blew our turbans off, but on we charged and plunged the white-hot spits into his red-rimmed, blue-lidded eyes.

The cannibal let out a yell like doomsday. We were thrown in all directions as the grotesque beast staggered to his knees and slapped the ground trying to squash us like flies. Because he could not see us, we were able to lean our makeshift ladder against the wall and climb out, pulling the benches over behind us, because they were to serve as our raft.

But we had no sooner pushed off from the shore, paddling

with our hands, than a female giant with the same dewlap cheeks, ears flapping as she ran, appeared on the beach leading the blinded cannibal by the hand. Truly the sight of them was so repulsive that the shallow shorelines waves wrinkled up their noses.

The giants stood howling at us from the beach, baring their fangs and barking as great black conger eels bark on the hook. Then they picked up boulders and threw them at the raft, swamping it with pitching waves and smashing some of our boards. Only three of us were left clinging to the raft when it drifted beyond range of the falling rocks, and limped out on to the open ocean.

For a day and a night we watched for land until our eyes were as dry as pebbles. And then we slept.

"Wake up, wake up!" I cried shortly before dawn. "The sea's as still as the milk in a cat's saucer. We must have entered a lagoon."

Lying on our raft, we waited for the sun to tell us what kind of land the sea had brought us to. Little by little, it lit a circle of scaly coral which totally enclosed the raft so that I could not tell how we had sailed inside. I was remarking on the multicolored scales of the reef, when the sea monster whose coils had surrounded us, lifted its multicolored head and sipped a sailor off the raft.

Round and round its coils writhed, spinning the raft in a whirlpool of snake. At night it was hidden by darkness. But its loud hissing made us long to hear waves breaking on Arabian beaches before we met our end. In the morning I was all alone. The sea serpent had licked my last companion off the deck and left me one more day in which to praise Allah.

It seemed time to act. I tore up the benches from the edge of the raft and raised wooden walls and a roof, so that I was floating in a lidded wooden box.

"At least if I am to die," said I, "Sinbad will have a respectable coffin as befits a Believer."

Round and round the sea snake wheeled, spinning the crate in a whirlpool of serpent. Then in the night it nosed me up and down, hissing like a punctured elephant, but truly it found Sinbad and his coffin an indigestible meal and swam off by first light to wreck the ships of Believers and Unbelievers alike. May Allah grant it a short life.

My flimsy box was sighted by a merchant ship. The sailors mistook it for a crate washed overboard from a cargo ship and were greatly amazed to pry open the lid and find a creature of my kind inside.

The sailors did not press me for my story, and I rested below-decks for several days, interested only in eating and sleeping, though they told me that I cried out in my sleep: "Oh, Allah, maroon me on the Island of Zughb, if I ever see Baghdad again and do not stay at home to grow old!"

"The captain is from Baghdad," said the second mate. "But we won't be docking there again. He will have to sell the ship at the next port we come to. Times are bad in shipping and he is nearly ruined." The sailor shook his head disappointedly. "And they say the captain has a rich cargo waiting in a Baghdad warehouse, but he won't sell it in case the owner comes back to claim it. Come back from the dead after seven years! Sinbad won't come back. He went down with a whale to the kingdom where only the fish can breathe."

I dropped from my hammock and begged them to take me to the captain. The old man did not recognize me at once, but I remembered his face so well as the ship pulled away from the whale-island, and his voice shouting "Aboard! Aboard! Or you are all dead men!"

I was so grateful to the good captain for keeping my cargo, that I gave him half its value and one of the ships that had found its way back from the far distant Diamond Valley. For I am almost embarrassed to tell you what wealth awaited me at home. My friends, the trade winds had shepherded my scattered fleet to Basra Harbor, and there the cargoes had been sold for more dinars than can be counted on an abacus.

The captain came to visit me here when he was in port, bringing stories from the liquid mountains of the sea where there are as many wonderful beasts and fabulous islands as there are trees in a forest. I was tempted, Allah forgive me, to set sail again on other voyages and I met with other adventures.

"But I have stolen too many moments from the span of your life," said Sinbad the Sailor to Sinbad the Porter. "May Allah reward you and all those who have an attentive ear and can listen with their hearts to an old man's stories."

Bobbi! Bobbi!

AUSTRALIA

In the Dream-time, when the world was still in the making, the Ancient Sleepers rose from their beds and walked across sea and land, shaping the rocks, the plants, the creatures, arranging the stars to please the eye.

I remember. Or if not I, an ancestor of mine, or if not he, a sister of his ancestor. Our memories are blurred now, but we do remember: how the Ancient Sleeping spirits walked the Earth during Dream-time, and made things ready for us.

The snake spirit, Bobbi Bobbi, on his walk, heard crying and came upon a group of human beings newly brought to life.

"Does the world not please you for a place to live?" he asked.

"It would please us," sobbed the people, "if we were not so *hungry!*"

So Bobbi Bobbi searched his dreams for a kind of food, then gave it shape from a handful of soil. He made one flying bat and then another. Big they were, and meaty, each one a meal to feed a family. By the time Bobbi Bobbi walked on his way, over the brand-new world, the sky behind him was black with bats.

Binbinga lit a fire. Banbangi his sister crept up on a bat where it hung by its toes from a tree.

Crackle-rattle! The bat heard her, for its hearing was sharp

and, just as she reached into the tree, it spread its leathery wings and flapped away.

Banbangi tended the fire. Binbinga took a stone and went to where the bats hung in a row by their toes from a cliff. He leaned back to throw.

Crackle-rattle! The bats heard him, for their hearing was keen, and just as he threw his stone, the bats spread their leathery wings and flapped away.

Bobbi Bobbi, walking home through the red light of evening, heard crying once again. Again, he came across the little new-made people—now looking more gaunt and desperate than before—and asked them what was wrong. But all they could do was point up at the sky at the flittering swarms of bats.

"We can't reach them. We can't catch them. All day we hunt them, but they won't be caught!"

Now Bobbi Bobbi was angry, because when he made a thing, he made it for a good purpose and not to find it fooling about in the red light of sunset. In his anger he beat his chest, till the ringing of his ribs gave him an idea.

With the sharp blade of the sickle moon, he cut a slit in the side of his chest, he reached in his hand, and pulled out a rib, a single rib. Taking a squinting aim on the circling bats, he flung the rib—it flew with a singing whistle—and tumbled a fine fat bat out of the blood-red sky!

The little people jumped and cheered, but not so high nor as loud as they jumped and cheered at what happened next. Bobbi Bobbi's rib-stick came whirling back out of the scarlet sky—right to his hand, right to the very palm of his hand!

Bobbi Bobbi gave his marvellous rib to the hungry newcomers and—wonder of wonders!—even when they threw it, it knocked the bats from the sky then swooped home again to their hands. "Boomerang," they called it, a treasure entrusted to them by the gods. A very piece of the gods.

No wonder they grew proud.

They knocked down more bats than they could eat, just to prove they could do it. The best throwers even boasted that they could knock down the birds…

"…the clouds…!"

"…the moon…!"

And as they strove to outdo one another, Binbinga threw the boomerang so hard and so high that he knocked a hole in the sky!

Down fell rubble and blue dust, onto the ground below. Winds escaped through the gap, stars showed at midday, and the handiwork of the Ancient Sleepers was spoiled.

Now Bobbi Bobbi was really angry, because when he made a thing, he made it to good purpose, not to see it played with by fools.

Before the boomerang could arc back through the tear in the sky, Bobbi Bobbi reared up, caught it in his mouth and shook it with rage.

"Quick! Before he swallows it!" cried Binbinga.

"He mustn't take it from us!" cried Banbangi. And they ran at the great snake spirit, scrambled up his scaly body, clambered up his trunk toward the broad, toothless rim of his mouth. They each took hold of one end of the precious boomerang. In their ignorance, they actually tried to pull it out of Bobbi Bobbi's mouth!

But the snake spirit only dislocated his jaw (as snakes can) to widen the gap of his cavernous jaw, and swallowed Binbinga and Banbangi, swallowed them whole.

A great silence fell over the newly made world, broken only by the *rattle-crack* of the last remaining bats.

For a long while, the flying bats cruised the sky above the new-made people. Daily they increased in number, just as the hunger increased in the bellies of those below. When, at last, Bobbi Bobbi relented and gave back the rib-stick, it was only in exchange for their promises to use it as it was meant to be used— for catching food.

The Namashepani

EAST AFRICA

"In the time of our grandmothers and grandfathers," began Mama Semamingi, "our people grew corn, too, just like we do now."

The children huddled in close around Mama Semamingi, because she always told good stories. Mama Semamingi was very old—at least as old as the gnarled wood of her cane—and she knew so much. She must have known all of the grandmothers and grandfathers she tells about in her stories, thought the children.

"One woman, Kanira, had an especially wonderful cornfield. When the corn was ripe, she and her daughter, Wanuki, gathered as much of the corn as they could into baskets. Carrying the baskets on their heads, they left the cornfield for home, Kanira in front and Wanuki behind on the narrow path. But as they were walking, Wanuki said to her mother, 'Mama, my basket is getting lighter and lighter with every step. I seem to have very little corn, but I know that I left the field with it full.'

"'Aiii, child, don't speak bad magic. People will call you a witch. I am sure that you only imagine your basket is lighter.'

"They continued walking through the corn and banana fields.

"'Mama,' cried Wanuki, 'something is taking my corn! I have almost nothing left in my basket.'

"'Oh, Wanuki, let me see.' Kanira sighed and turned to peer

into her daughter's basket. She gasped and said, 'Wanuki, you are right! You have almost no corn left. The cobs are still there, but something is picking off all of the kernels.'

"'How could something only take the kernels, without me noticing?' asked Wanuki somewhat fearfully. 'I think I would hear and see an animal crawling into my basket.'

"'I don't know. Let's keep walking, but this time, I will stay behind you.' Kanira, who was taller, watched Wanuki's basket closely all the way home, but this time nothing came to steal the corn.

"The next day, Wanuki and Kanira again went to the cornfield to fill their baskets. Once they were back on the narrow path home, Kanira said, 'Wanuki, walk in front of me again. Your corn seems to be safe if I watch it.'

"When they were close to the place where Wanuki first said that her basket was lighter, Kanira cried, 'Aiii, my basket is getting lighter! The thief is stealing from me too.'

"'Mama, let me see your basket.' When Kanira put her basket down, they both gasped. All of the cobs were picked clean. Every kernel was gone.

"'Let's go home quickly,' said Kanira, 'and tell your father.'

"'Yes, maybe he can catch whoever is taking our corn,' said Wanuki.

"After the family had eaten that night, and when they were all sitting quietly around the fire, Kanira said to her husband, 'Ganui, something is taking our corn, right from our baskets.'

"'What do you mean, Kanira? How can something steal corn from your baskets?'

"'It is as I tell you. Yesterday, as Wanuki and I were walking from the cornfield, we noticed that something had picked the kernels off many of the cobs....'

"'How...?' interrupted Ganui, puzzled.

"'And, today,' continued Kanira, 'I walked behind Wanuki to watch her basket, but then every cob was stripped bare in my basket.'

"'You must be bewitched!' exclaimed Ganui. 'How can something fly or crawl into your basket without you or Wanuki noticing?' Wanuki and Kanira exchanged glances, not knowing what to say. 'Never mind, tomorrow I will go with you to the cornfield. Maybe I can scare away this thief.'

"The next day, Ganui, Kanira, and Wanuki, with their baskets full, followed in a line along the narrow path from the cornfield. Kanira and Wanuki were in front and Ganui stayed a little behind. Sometimes Ganui would duck in bushes and behind trees, trying to fool the corn-kernel thieves into thinking that his wife and daughter were alone.

"They had only walked a little way, when Ganui shouted, 'Jambo, little man, how are you?'

"Kanira and Wanuki both cried, 'What!' at the same time, and turned immediately to see what had happened to Ganui.

"Ganui smiled and said, 'One of our little people, but he has flown away.'

"Now Kanira was confused. She said, 'What do you mean, Ganui? What are these little people? Are you playing tricks on me and your daughter?'

"'I swear on my heart, my lovely wife, that I would never play tricks on you.' Ganui smiled. 'Didn't your grandmothers ever tell you about the little people?'

"'Tell me about the little people, Papa,' said Wanuki.

"'The one I saw looked just as my grandmother told me. He was no taller than my forearm and he had thin, colorful wings, like a butterfly.'

"'Wings?' Wanuki's eyes were big with wonder.

"'Yes, he flew straight into your basket. And with a tiny golden hammer that he carried in his left hand, he chipped away at the kernels on the corncobs. His clothes were white like cobwebs and he had long, black hair. Grandmother said the little people grow their hair long to sweep away their footsteps when they walk. She also said the little people dry their clothes in hillsides early in the morning. Wanuki, surely you have seen the little people's clothes?'

"'I have seen them,' replied Wanuki, 'but I would like to see one of these little people. Can we catch one, Papa?'

"'I think if we sit here quietly beside the path, we will see one of them,' said Ganui.

"As the family waited beside the path, they talked about the little people. Kanira, too, remembered some of her grandmother's stories.

"'When I was really young, my grandmother told about her friend that was taken away to live with the little people. She was

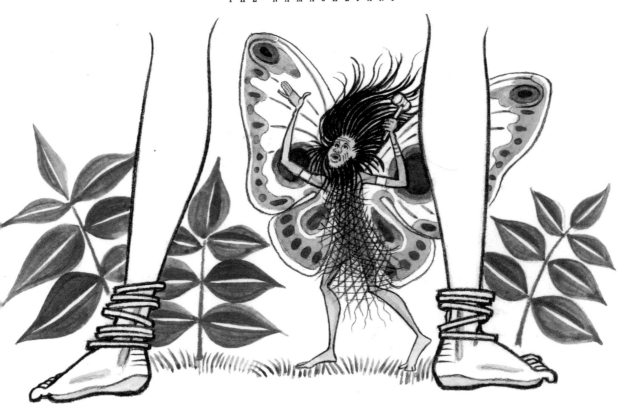

sleeping in the shade on a warm day. A little later, my grandmother saw her talking to a little person, and then, all of a sudden she was gone. Nobody ever saw my grandmother's friend again.'

"'Terrible! Are the little people bad?' asked Wanuki.

"'No, they are not so terrible. People say they are happy. They wash their clothes by moonlight, and when it rains, they sing and dance. They do sometimes steal people's food, like corn and peanuts, when they grow tired of collecting berries and drinking from rain puddles.'

"'Do the little people have a name, Mama?' asked Wanuki.

"'They are called the Namashepani.'

"'Jambo, hello. You called me, Kanira.' A voice like a tiny bell called up to them. On the path before Kanira, Ganui, and Wanuki stood a little man. He looked just as Ganui had described him, with butterfly wings and long black hair.

"'I only said your name!' said Kanira, flabbergasted. 'How do you know mine?'

"The Namashepani bowed. 'My name is enough to bring me, and your name is among many, many things I know.'

"'Oh you are so small, little man!' exclaimed Wanuki.

"The Namashepani bowed again and said, 'Kanira, how tall do I seem to you?'

"'You are very small, little man.'

"The Namashepani flashed a wicked grin and turned to Ganui. 'And you, Ganui, how tall do you think I am?'

"'You are no longer than my forearm. You are very small, little man.'

"The Namashepani smiled again, but not happily. 'Now I will tell you three about me,' he said. 'The Namashepani do not hurt people, and, yes, sometimes we steal your food, but we do not like to be so small. Anybody who calls us little will become as small as we are.' The Namashepani quickly flew up to the family before they could say anything else, and he tapped them sharply on their heads with his golden hammer.

"Kanira, Ganui, and Wanuki shrunk, their clothing falling off around them. Soon, they were small like the Namashepani. Their wings unfolded and the Namashepani beckoned them to follow him to the hillsides where the other little people lived. Kanira, Ganui, and Wanuki wash their clothes by moonlight now, and sometimes they come down from their hillside home to steal corn from the harvesters' baskets.

"If you ever meet a little person, my children," said Mama Semamingi solemnly, "tell him that he is bwana mkubwa, a very big man, or he will hit you with his hammer and you will become a Namashepani."

The Theft of Fire

CHIPEWYAN

It was back in the time when the manitou spirits still lived freely among the Indian people that fire disappeared. It was gone for so long, there were many who had never felt its flame.

The winter had descended suddenly on Manabozho. It was the first year of his manhood and he stood impatiently before his grandmother's wigwam, shivering in the cold, cruel wind. There was no warmth to be had from the pale yellow sun. The earth was covered in snow and the lake was frozen. Manabozho knew that for many months his lodge would be cold, his food frozen, and his drinking water underneath four feet of solid ice.

"Aaah, Nakomis, old grandmother," he said sadly, "it is another cold winter that is upon us. How I wish I could capture the warmth of the sun!"

Nakomis looked up from her sewing and smiled at her strong grandson. "Once, long ago, we did have warmth in our wigwams, even through the winter. But this was a long time ago," she replied.

"I have heard of this warmth that lasts even in winter. Is it true?"

"You have heard of fire," his grandmother replied.

"What is this fire," asked Manabozho, "that keeps men warm?"

Nakomis looked quietly at her grandson for a moment before she tried to answer his question. "It is like the sun," she said at last.

"It is like having a small sun inside the lodge to keep us warm. You must tend this sun with wood to keep it burning. When it is small, it needs small sticks and birchbark to grow larger. When it is large it can eat whole trees."

"How do you know of this fire, Nakomis?"

"Once, long ago, all men had fire, but it was taken from them. Now one old crippled man guards over what is left so that no other lodge shall have it."

"Do you know where the old man lives that I can get this fire to warm us?"

"You cannot get it, Manabozho. It is far across the ice, watched day and night by the old man."

"But the old man must eat," Manabozho said. "I will get it while he is out!"

"You cannot, Manabozho. He never leaves the fire, for he is nearly blind and crippled. He lives with his two daughters and it is their job to feed both him and the fire. They fetch the wood, the water and they set traps for the food. The fire is never left alone."

"It does not seem so hard to get fire from a crippled blind man and his two squaws who are not always in the wigwam. If I try, surely I will get it!"

"It is so hard, Manabozho, it can never be," his grandmother replied. "All day long the old man sits by the fire and weaves a great net to catch anyone who comes near him or his daughters. No one can get to the fire. You will fail."

"Nevertheless, I shall get the fire," said Manabozho. "Go and gather whatever it is you need to feed it. I will bring the fire to you."

Manabozho reached for his rabbit-skin robe and wrapped it carefully around him. He stepped out into the darkness and looked across the frozen lake. He could not see the other shore. The cold wind reached out to sting his cheeks and wrap its icy fingers around him. But Manabozho simply bowed his head and started across the freshly frozen ice in the direction of the old man's wigwam.

The lake stretched out smooth and slippery in front of him. Stepping carefully, Manabozho walked slowly upon its delicate surface. He watched for air holes that let the water underneath flow up to freeze around the edges in a rough, white stretch. Sometimes his weight sent rapidly moving cracks zigzagging across the ice from beneath his feet. The sound of the ice cracking beneath him was like thunder booming across the sky. But Manabozho did not fear, for he knew the ice was already four fingers thick and growing thicker each hour. As long as he took care to avoid the air holes, the ice would hold him.

As the night wrapped itself around him, little white snow-flakes began to drift from the sky. The wind made the snowflakes look like they were dancing around him. Soon, though, the snow began to fall much harder and Manabozho could no longer see the shore behind him. The wind blew harder and the night grew colder. He wondered how much farther the old man's wigwam could be. It could not be much farther! It was easy to lose one's direction in such a fierce, cold storm.

And then, at last! He knew he was near. He had reached the hole in the lake ice into which the old man's daughters dipped their buckets for their drinking water.

"Now," said Manabozho, "I must be near their lodge. They will never let me near. I must change myself to something that a young squaw will wish to take inside the wigwam."

As he spoke, his rabbit-skin robe began to move more closely around him, until he had become one with the skin. Soon, he had become one of his favorite disguises. He hopped across the ice and shivered beside the water hole. Manabozho the manitou, the great spirit, had become Manabozho the hare. Though, as he shivered in the night, there was nothing great about his appearance. He looked to be just a small, cold, and frightened little rabbit.

After what seemed to be a very long time of waiting, a woman emerged from the lodge, carrying a birchbark bucket. Manabozho quickly broke through the half-formed ice and jumped into the freezing cold water of the ice hole. He immediately began to splutter and choke as though he were drowning.

The squaw heard the noise and ran quickly to look into the hole. Using her pail, she dipped him from the water. "Oh! You poor little rabbit!" she said, taking him from the bucket and holding him close.

Manabozho coughed and shivered in her arms. His wet fur was quickly freezing in the night's cold air. He was finding it far

nicer being in the pretty squaw's warm arms than floundering about in the ice water of the hole.

"You poor little thing," she said, wrapping her robe carefully around him, "I shall take you into the lodge and my sister and I will dry you and warm you before the fire." Holding him with one hand and using the other to fill the bucket half full with water, she then carried Manabozho to her father and sister inside the wigwam.

Once inside she looked quickly across the lodge to the sleeping old man in the corner and then gave a sigh of relief. Turning to her sister she said quietly, "Look at what I have found drowning in our water hole. We must dry him and warm him before he dies from the cold. Here, you hold him while I tend the fire. Be careful not to wake father!" and she thrust Manabozho into the older woman's arms.

Though it was dark inside the lodge, Manabozho could see that this squaw was neither so young nor so pretty as the one who had rescued him from the water. She held him loosely with her hands stretched out in front of her and half-turned fearfully toward the figure in the corner of the wigwam. Manabozho also looked and saw that the father continued to sleep. "He will not like it," the older squaw said, her head nodding in the direction of the old man. She held her lips together quite severely and unconsciously pinched Manabozho.

"But he is such a sweet little thing, so cold and helpless," the younger sister said and reached out her arms to take him.

Manabozho did not like the way he was being held and began to squirm and wriggle in the older sister's arms, anxious to return to the prettier sister. But the older woman neither dropped him nor returned him but instead drew him close and cradled him against her. She slowly began to stroke his trembling wet fur. At last she smiled. "Poor little thing!" she said. "Do stop your shaking." She turned toward her sister. "Perhaps Father will let us keep him." And she continued to smile as she petted Manabozho.

Secure in her arms, Manabozho finally decided to look around the wigwam in search of the fire. There, lying between two logs, glowing a dull red, the color of the sun as the night began to fall, and now and then shooting out yellow arrows, the color of the sun during the day, was the fire he had come to steal. It glowed brightly, casting soft shadows upon the walls of the lodge.

Suddenly the old man stirred upon his bed of skins. Waking, he pulled a pair of crippled legs from beneath him and looked about.

"What stranger has been here while I have been sleeping?" he asked crossly. He pulled a great net from the floor and began weaving new strands across it, knotting them firmly. "I must make this net bigger and stronger and throw it over him when he comes again."

"Oh, Father," said the older sister calmly, "No one has been here at all."

"Oh?" he replied turning toward her gaze. "I think a stranger has." He paused and said forcefully, "I think he is here still."

The elder sister held the rabbit out before her. "Is this what you fear, Father?" she asked softly. "It is only a wet little rabbit that we found in the water hole. You need not fear this rabbit."

The old man stopped his work to look at Manabozho. "I thought it was a man," he said, quietly squinting as he looked toward the rabbit. "But how do you know that is not a manitou who has turned himself into a rabbit? Manitous can take the shape and voices of animals! He may have come to the lodge to steal our fire!"

"Oh! Father!" cried the two girls, together.

The fire glowed softly between father and daughters, and Manabozho almost smiled, thinking how simple it would be to steal a spark from its flames and take it home to Nakomis. It would make their lodge warm and comfortable like this one.

"He is really just a rabbit," said the elder daughter.

"He is just a cold, wet rabbit," added the younger. "Let us keep him by the fire and warm him!"

Manabozho squirmed once again in the elder sister's arms, so anxious was he to get to the fire and then away.

"Well, if he really is a rabbit .... But if he steals our fire ...."

"Him?" The elder sister held Manabozho before her, toward the fire. "How could this little thing steal anything at all? And why should it matter if he did? We would still have much left." The glowing embers were just beneath Manabozho now. He wondered whether his fur was dry enough to take a spark.

"Then the others would have it as well as we," observed the father.

"Why would that matter?"

"Ach! You are but a girl. Yet you should still know that when you have something that others want, that something gives you a power over them. But warm your rabbit if you must, just hope that he is only a rabbit."

"I still do not understand—" said the younger daughter.

"Of course you do not! Listen, woman. If those from another lodge can take our fire from us, they will not sit and watch the flames. Soon they will recall that we have other things, and they will come and try to take them from us as well, just as they did with our fire. But warm the rabbit, if you wish. I will say no more."

Kneeling before the fire, the girls laid Manabozho down and brushed his back until his fur was once again dry and soft to the touch. They then turned him over and warmed his underside until he was white and fluffy, petting and stroking him.

"He is very soft," said the elder.

"We shall keep him to play with," said the younger.

"You had better plan to eat him!" said the father.

Just then Manabozho rolled over to the embers and picked up a spark in the soft, dry fur upon his back. No sooner than he could feel the soft burning than he was out of the lodge and streaking back across the ice. The speed of his flight and the cold wind fanned the spark upon his back into a flame.

The old man struggled to his feet and hobbled to the doorway of his wigwam. He stood watching the tiny light disappear across the frozen lake. The great net hung useless in his arms.

"Just as I feared, that was a manitou, not a rabbit. The manitous are very powerful and will take odd shapes to get the things they want. Now some other lodge will have fire again."

Across the ice Manabozho was nearing his grandmother's wigwam, a great flame upon his back, nearly to his tail. Though his back ached, he would not stop and roll in the snow. He kept running onward, calling as he came.

"Noko! Noko!" he cried. "Have your sticks ready, for I bring you a hungry fire!"

Manabozho's grandmother held the door of the lodge open for him to enter. Quickly she rubbed a piece of birch bark onto the burning fur, blew until it burst into flame, laid it upon the ground and began to add tiny splinters of wood. As the flame grew larger, she laid on twigs and branches until a beautiful warm rosy glow burned brightly in the cold lodge.

Manabozho was busy rolling back and forth upon the earth floor, putting out the sparks that still clung to his smoldering hide.

When Nakomis had the fire burning brightly, she turned to look at her grandson. He was standing in the wigwam, rubbing the burned spots up and down his backbone.

"Well," she said, "you did it. I did not think you could."

"Of course I did!" shouted Manabozho proudly. "But my back is scorched and sore. And look! Most of my fur is gone. Why do you just sit there looking at me?"

"You are a fool!" said Nakomis, turning from him with a small smile upon her face.

"But why am I a fool when I—"

"Because it is only the rabbit skin that is burned."

"I don't see—"

Nakomis sighed. "Are you a Manabozho or a rabbit?" she asked.

"I am Manabozho, of course! Don't I look like Manabozho?"

"No," she replied, "You look like a rabbit. Why don't you change yourself back into Manabozho? Then perhaps your back will not hurt."

Manabozho now understood why he had been foolish. Quickly he turned himself back into an Indian and, sure enough, his skin was not hurt. Neither was his hair scorched. What he did have, however, was a slightly scorched rabbit skin draped around his shoulders.

He dropped the robe before the lodge fire. Already he could feel its warmth spreading throughout the wigwam. He sat down and began to think about what else he'd seen in the old man's lodge. He smiled when he remembered the pretty young squaw. The old man's net too; it might be used for fishing. The pile of skins in the corner would be good for sleeping. And the daughter. If he was ever to have his own lodge he would need someone like her to make it comfortable and pleasant. Manabozho smiled slyly as he began to plan a way he could get her to leave her father and sister, and come and live with him and old Nakomis.

The Yellow Thunder Dragon

CHINA

Once, a very long time ago, there was a quiet, thoughtful young boy named Chang. Chang would often spend his time looking about his world and dreaming that something wonderful and extraordinary would happen to him and change his life. Nothing ever did, though...until one day when he was just thirteen years old.

Chang lived on a farm with his father, Yin, and his grandmother. His grandmother was very special. She was old and wise, and she looked carefully after Chang, giving him lots of extra love, for his mother had died when he was a baby.

One hot afternoon, when Grandmother lay sleeping in the afternoon heat, and Father was busy working inside the house, Chang wandered out to the garden gate to look across at the rolling fields and winding river to the valley that lay beyond. He was quietly daydreaming when he noticed a handsome young man riding up the road on what looked to be a white horse. He was dressed all in yellow and he had four menservants walking along beside him. One of the servants held a splendid yellow umbrella over the young man's head to shade him from the sun. There was something strange about these travelers.

Chang watched them carefully. The horse, as it moved closer, seemed to shimmer in the afternoon light. It was like watching sunshine dappling across the water. Chang was sure its hooves didn't touch the ground. The menservants' feet didn't touch the ground, either. It was as if the whole group were walking upon air.

The travelers drew closer to the gate. When they reached Chang, they stopped and the young man looked down from his shimmering horse and said, "I am weary, Chang, son of Yin. May I enter your father's garden and rest?"

Chang bowed low before the stranger and swung open the gate. "Please enter, my lord," he said.

The group entered through the gates and after the young man had swung down from his horse, a servant tethered it to the gatepost. Then they all went and sat down in the courtyard, next to the house.

Chang's father came out of the house when he heard the sound of voices in the courtyard. He welcomed the strangers to his home and asked Chang to bring out some refreshments. He then sat opposite the handsome stranger and they began to talk.

As the strangers settled in for their afternoon rest, Chang stood off to the side and watched them carefully, his arms folded around him. He noticed that the handsome stranger's clothes had no seams, but appeared to be woven entirely out of one piece of cloth. And his feet did not touch the ground when he walked. Chang then looked closely at the stranger's horse and saw that its body was not covered in hair, as other horses were, but rather in small white shiny scales, each of which held five tiny perfect spots of color that shone and sparkled in the sun.

Once the travelers were finished eating and drinking, they rose from the table, and the young man thanked Yin graciously for his hospitality. They then took their leave. As they walked across the gateway, Chang noticed that the servant who was carrying the splendid yellow umbrella turned it upside down before crossing the gateway. Upon reaching the road, he turned it right-side up once again.

"I shall return again tomorrow," the handsome young man said to Chang.

"As you wish, my lord," Chang answered, bowing.

Chang watched as the strangers rode away from the farm. They rode up the road toward the mountains. They climbed higher and higher until, suddenly, they rose into the air and vanished into the rain clouds that were gathering above the mountains.

When Chang returned to the house, his father said, "What strange visitors! I've never seen the young man before, and yet he knew my name and everything about me. Did you not notice anything unusual about our guests?"

"Yes, Father, I did. Neither their feet nor the horse's hooves touched the ground, and—"

"Their feet did not touch the ground!" exclaimed Yin. "Then they were spirits, not men. We must tell your grandmother at once. She knows much about the spirit world."

Grandmother lay in a deep sleep when Chang and his father approached. She would not wake up when they called to her. At last, she stirred and yawned.

"Grandmother," said Chang, "there were strange visitors here today whose feet did not touch the ground."

Chang's grandmother blinked, and was immediately alert. "Tell me about them," she said.

Chang told her about the handsome young man and his yellow

seamless clothes; his four servants; and the strange, magical horse. He told her that, when they left, they rose into the air and disappeared among the clouds.

"Seamless clothes are magic clothes," said Grandmother. "And yellow is a sacred color. The young man must have been the Yellow Thunder Dragon. His horse is the dragon horse, and the servants are the four winds. This means a great storm will soon come...." She frowned. "Is there nothing else you can tell me?" she asked.

"There is nothing else," Chang said slowly, thinking. Then: "The servant who carried the umbrella turned it upside down before leaving our garden."

"That is a good omen," said Grandmother. Then she closed her eyes once again and fell into a deep sleep.

That evening Yin looked out and saw dark thunder clouds gathering above the mountains. He decided that he and Chang would stay up and wait for the storm. Chang decided to put on a yellow robe that his grandmother had made for him to honor the Yellow Thunder Dragon. He also lit a yellow lantern and burned incense and read magic charms from an ancient yellow book.

Meanwhile, Grandmother slept.

It was only much later that night that the storm finally broke. Chang closed his book and, together with his father, looked out the window at the great storm. Lightning lit up the sky like a torch. Thunder rolled and boomed. And down came the heaving rain. The streams swelled and gushed from the onslaught. The river rose higher and higher until it burst, raging, from its banks and flooded the fields, sweeping away all in its path—trees, houses and even living creatures.

Time passed. The thunder grew to a quiet rumble and the lightning moved away. But still the rain came down. When it grew light, Yin opened the door and he and Chang looked out across their field; they could see that the flood water reached right up to their garden.

"Aah, Chang," Yin said sadly, "we should have fled to the mountains last night. We would have been safe there. Now it is too late."

Chang stepped out into the garden and looked up to the sky. Above their house he saw the yellow dragon, with its hood spread out as if to protect them from the rain. For one brief moment it was there—and then it was gone.

"Father!" he cried. "I have seen the Yellow Thunder Dragon!"

"You are tired, my son," said Yin.

"But look, Father! It is not raining upon our house!" exclaimed Chang.

And sure enough, when Yin went out he saw for himself that, though it rained everywhere else, no rain fell upon their roof.

"The Thunder Dragon is protecting us," he said. "It was fortunate that you welcomed him yesterday, my son."

Later that afternoon the rain stopped. It was only then that Yin and his son realized the extent to which they had been protected. In all the plain, it was their house, and their house alone, that had remained undamaged from the storm. The flood waters had come right up to their garden and then parted to sweep around it, as if held back by a strong invisible wall.

When the sun finally came out Chang went to stand, once again, by the garden gate. He looked to the west and saw the young man, dressed all in yellow and mounted on his shimmering horse. He rode down from the mountains with his four servants. As before, their feet did not touch the ground. They stopped at the garden gate.

"I told you I would come again," the young man said. "This time I shall not enter your garden."

Chang bowed, "Whatever you wish," he said.

The young man took a scale from the horse's neck and gave it to Chang. "Keep this safe," he said. "And use it wisely."

Chang took the gift and bowed once again.

The young man and his servants continued on their way. They traveled across the flood water, and the horse's hooves and the servants' feet seemed to walk on air. On and on they went, and then, suddenly, they sank down into the water and vanished.

Chang hurried inside and placed the scale from the horse's neck in a small wooden box lined with silk. Then he went to his father and told him that the Yellow Thunder Dragon had returned to his pool.

"We must tell Grandmother," said Yin.

Grandmother *still* lay asleep. But at last when she stirred and opened her eyes, Chang told her about the great storm and the young man's return visit, and he showed her small shiny scale.

"Now when the Emperor sends for you both," said Grandmother, "all will be well."

"Why would the Emperor send for us?" asked Yin.

"You shall see," she said. And with that she closed her eyes and was again asleep.

It was not very long before the Emperor heard news of the great flood and of the strange marvel that had been seen by those who'd fled to the moutains to escape the storm. He heard stories of the rain that fell everywhere but for one house, the house of Yin the farmer—and the flood waters that had swept around his house and garden, as if they were protected by a strong and invisible wall.

The Emperor thought there must be some powerful magic at work there, and so he sent messengers with orders that Yin and all who lived within his house should come to the imperial palace.

Well, Chang and his father tried to get Grandmother to go, but she refused. She said she wanted to sleep. So Chang and his father set off at once.

It was early evening by the time they reached the imperial palace. The Emperor received them at once and asked Yin to tell him all that had happened during the storm.

"My lord," said Yin, "the story belongs to my son, Chang. He is the one who must tell it."

So Chang told the story of the Yellow Thunder Dragon. By the time he got to the end it was dark. Then he took the small shiny scale out of its silk-lined box, and it shone so brightly it lit up the throne room like the sun.

"Chang, son of Yin," said the Emperor, "you shall remain here and become one of my royal magicians, for the Yellow Thunder

Dragon has given you a scale that holds within it strong magical powers."

And so it came to be that Chang, though he was only thirteen years old, became the Emperor's royal magician; and as time passed he found that, indeed, there was powerful magic in the scale from the dragon horse. With this magic scale he found he could heal the sick and foretell the future. He could even win mighty victories for the emperor's army.

In return for Chang's great magic, the Emperor rewarded him with a great house near the imperial palace; and his father and grandmother came and lived with him there.

His father lived the comfortable life of a rich lord. And Grandmother? Well, she *still* slept most of the time. But when she did wake, she shared with Chang the wisdom and knowledge of her many years.

The Orphan Boy and the Elk Dog

AMERICAN INDIAN (BLACKFOOT)

In the days when people had only dogs to carry their bundles, two orphan children, a boy and his sister, were having a hard time. The boy was deaf, and because he could not understand what people said, they thought him foolish and dull-witted. Even his relatives wanted nothing to do with him. The name he had been given at birth, while his parents still lived, was Long Arrow. Now he was like a beaten, mangy dog, the kind who hungrily roams outside a camp, circling it from afar, smelling the good meat boiling in the kettles but never coming close for fear of being kicked. Only his sister, who was bright and beautiful, loved him.

Then the sister was adopted by a family from another camp, people who were attracted by her good looks and pleasing ways. Though they wanted her for a daughter, they certainly did not want the awkward, stupid boy. And so they took away the only person who cared about him, and the orphan boy was left to fend for himself. He lived on scraps thrown to the dogs and things he found on the refuse heaps. He dressed in remnants of skins and frayed robes discarded by the poorest people. At night he bedded down in a grass-lined dugout, like an animal in its den.

Eventually the game was eliminated near the camp that the boy regarded as his, and the people decided to move. The lodges were taken down, belongings were packed into rawhide bags and put on dog sleds, and the village departed. "Stay here," they told the boy. "We don't want your kind coming with us."

For two or three days the boy fed on scraps the people had left behind, but he knew he would starve if he stayed. He had to join his people, whether they liked it or not. He followed their tracks, frantic that he would lose them, and crying at the same time. Soon the sweat was running down his skinny body. As he was stumbling, running, panting, something suddenly snapped in his left ear with a sound like a small crack, and a wormlike substance came out of that ear. All at once on his left side he could hear birdsongs for the first time. He took this wormlike thing in his left hand and hurried on. Then there was a snap in his right ear and a wormlike thing came out of it, and on his right side he could hear the rushing waters of a stream. His hearing was restored! And it was razor-sharp—he could make out the rustling of a tiny mouse in dry leaves a good distance away. The orphan boy laughed and was happy for the first time in his life. With renewed courage he followed the trail his people had made.

In the meantime the village had settled into its new place. Men were already out hunting. Thus the boy came upon Good Running, a kindly old chief, butchering a fat buffalo cow he had just killed. When the chief saw the boy, he said to himself, "Here comes that poor good-for-nothing boy. It was wrong to abandon him." To the boy Good Running said, "Rest here, Grandson, you're sweaty and covered with dust. Here, have some tripe."

The boy wolfed down the meat. He was not used to hearing

and talking yet, but his eyes were alert and Good Running also noticed a change in his manner. "This boy," the chief said to himself, "is neither stupid nor crazy." He gave the orphan a piece of the hump meat, then a piece of liver, then a piece of raw kidney, and at last the very best kind of meat—a slice of tongue. The more the old man looked at the boy, the more he liked him. On the spur of the moment he said, "Grandson, I'm going to adopt you; there's a place for you in my tipi. And I'm going to make you into a good hunter and warrior." The boy wept, this time for joy. Good Running said, "They called you a stupid, crazy boy, but now that I think of it, the name you were given at birth is Long Arrow. I'll see that people call you by your right name. Now come along."

The chief's wife was not pleased. "Why do you put this burden on me," she said, "bringing into our lodge this good-for-nothing, this slow-witted crazy boy? Maybe you're a little slow-witted and crazy yourself!"

"Woman, keep talking like that and I'll beat you! This boy isn't slow or crazy; he's a good boy, and I have taken him for my grandson. Look—he's barefooted. Hurry up and make a pair of moccasins for him, and if you don't do it well I'll take a stick to you."

Good Running's wife grumbled but did as she was told. Her husband was a kind man, but when aroused, his anger was great.

So a new life began for Long Arrow. He had to learn to speak and to understand well, and to catch up on all the things a boy should know. He was a fast learner and soon surpassed other boys his age in knowledge and skills. At last even Good Running's wife accepted him.

He grew up into a fine young hunter, tall and good-looking in the quilled buckskin outfit the chief's wife made for him. He helped his grandfather in everything and became a staff for Good Running to lean on. But he was lonely, for most people in the camp could not forget that Long Arrow had once been an outcast. "Grandfather," he said one day, "I want to do something to make you proud and show people that you were wise to adopt me. What can I do?"

Good Running answered, "Someday you will be a chief and do great things."

"But what's a great thing I could do now, Grandfather?"

The chief thought for a long time. "Maybe I shouldn't tell you this," he said. "I love you and don't want to lose you. But on winter nights, men talk of powerful spirit people living at the bottom of a faraway lake. Down in that lake the spirit people

keep mystery animals who do their work for them. These animals are larger than a great elk, but they carry the burdens of the spirit people like dogs. So they're called Pono-Kamita—Elk Dogs. They are said to be swift, strong, gentle, and beautiful beyond imagination. Every fourth generation, one of our young warriors has gone to find these spirit folk and bring back an Elk Dog for us. But none of our brave young men has ever returned."

"Grandfather, I'm not afraid. I'll go and find the Elk Dog."

"Grandson, first learn to be a man. Learn the right prayers and ceremonies. Be brave. Be generous and open-handed. Pity the old and the fatherless, and let the holy men of the tribe find a medicine for you that will protect you on your dangerous journey. We will begin by purifying you in the sweat bath."

So Long Arrow was purified with the white steam of the sweat lodge. He was taught how to use the pipe, and how to pray to the Great Mystery Power. The tribe's holy men gave him a medicine and made for him a shield with designs on it to ward off danger.

Then one morning, without telling anybody, Good Running loaded his best sled dog with all the things Long Arrow would need for traveling. The chief gave him his medicine, his shield, and his own fine bow and, just as the sun came up, went with his grandson to the edge of the camp to purify him with sweet-smelling cedar smoke. Long Arrow left unheard and unseen by anyone else. After a while some people noticed that he was gone, but no one except his grandfather knew where and for what purpose.

Following Good Running's advice, Long Arrow wandered southward. On the fourth day of his journey he came to a small pond, where a strange man was standing as if waiting for him. "Why have you come here?" the stranger asked.

"I have come to find the mysterious Elk Dog."

"Ah, there I cannot help you," said the man, who was the spirit of the pond. "But if you travel further south, four-times-four days, you might chance upon a bigger lake and there meet one of my uncles. Possibly he might talk to you; then again, he might not. That's all I can tell you."

Long Arrow thanked the man, who went down to the bottom of the pond, where he lived.

Long Arrow wandered on, walking for long hours and taking little time for rest. Through deep canyons and over high mountains he went, wearing out his moccasins and enduring cold and heat, hunger and thirst.

Finally, Long Arrow approached a big lake surrounded by steep, pine-covered hills. There he came face to face with a tall man, fierce and scowling and twice the height of most humans. This stranger carried a long lance with a heavy spearpoint made of shining flint. "Young one," he growled, "why did you come here?"

"I came to find the mysterious Elk Dog."

The stranger, who was the spirit of the lake, stuck his face right into Long Arrow's and shook his mighty lance. "Little one, aren't you afraid of me?" he snarled.

"No, I am not," answered Long Arrow, smiling.

The tall spirit man gave a hideous grin, which was his way of being friendly. "I like small humans who aren't afraid," he said, "but I can't help you. Perhaps our grandfather will take the trouble to listen to you. More likely he won't. Walk south for four-times-four days, and maybe you'll find him. But probably you won't." With that the tall spirit turned his back on Long Arrow and went to the bottom of the lake, where he lived.

Long Arrow walked on for another four-times-four days, sleeping and resting little. By now he staggered and stumbled in his weakness, and his dog was not much better off. At last he came to the biggest lake he had ever seen, surrounded by towering snow-capped peaks and waterfalls of ice. This time there was nobody to receive him. As a matter of fact, there seemed to be no living thing around. "This must be the Great Mystery Lake," thought Long Arrow. Exhausted, he fell down upon the shortgrass meadow by the lake, fell down among the wild flowers, and went to sleep with his tired dog curled up at his feet.

When Long Arrow awoke, the sun was already high. He opened his eyes and saw a beautiful child standing before him, a boy in a dazzling white buckskin robe decorated with porcupine quills of many colors. The boy said, "We have been expecting you for a long time. My grandfather invites you to his lodge. Follow me."

Telling his dog to wait, Long Arrow took his medicine shield and his grandfather's bow and went with the wonderful child. They came to the edge of the lake. The spirit boy pointed to the water and said, "My grandfather's lodge is down there. Come!" The child turned himself into a kingfisher and dove straight to the bottom.

Afraid, Long Arrow thought, "How can I follow him and not be drowned?" But then he said to himself, "I knew all the time that this would not be easy. In setting out to find the Elk Dog, I already threw my life away." And he boldly jumped into the water. To his surprise, he found it did not make him wet, that it parted before him, that he could breathe and see. He touched the lake's sandy bottom. It sloped down, down toward a center point.

Long Arrow descended this slope until he came to a small flat valley. In the middle of it stood a large tipi of tanned buffalo hide. The images of two strange animals were drawn on it in sacred vermilion paint. A kingfisher perched high on the top of the tipi flew down and turned again into the beautiful boy, who said, "Welcome. Enter my grandfather's lodge."

Long Arrow followed the spirit boy inside. In the back at the seat of honor sat a black-robed old man with flowing white hair and such power emanating from him that Long Arrow felt himself in the presence of a truly Great One. The holy man welcomed Long Arrow and offered him food. The man's wife came in bringing dishes of buffalo hump; liver; tongues; delicious chunks of deer meat; the roasted flesh of strange, tasty water birds; and meat pounded together with berries, chokecherries and kidney fat. Famished after his long journey, Long Arrow ate with relish. Yet he still looked around to admire the furnishings of the tipi, the painted inner curtain, the many medicine shields, wonderfully wrought weapons, shirts and robes decorated with porcupine quills in rainbow colors, beautifully painted rawhide containers filled with wonderful things, and much else that dazzled him.

After Long Arrow had stilled his hunger, the old spirit chief filled the pipe and passed it to his guest. They smoked, praying silently. After a while the old man said, "Some came before you from time to time, but they were always afraid of the deep water, and so they went away with empty hands. But you, grandson, were brave enough to plunge in, and therefore you are chosen to receive a wonderful gift to carry back to your people. Now, go outside with my grandson."

The beautiful boy took Long Arrow to a meadow on which some strange animals, unlike any the young man had ever seen, were galloping and gamboling, neighing and nickering. They were truly wonderful to look at, with their glossy coats fine as a maiden's hair, their long manes and tails streaming in the wind. Now rearing, now nuzzling, they looked at Long Arrow with gentle eyes that belied their fiery appearance.

"At last," thought Long Arrow, "here they are before my own eyes, the Pono-Kamita, the Elk Dogs!"

"Watch me," said the mystery boy, "so that you learn to do what I am doing." Gracefully and without effort, the boy swung himself onto the back of a jet-black Elk Dog with a high, arched neck. Larger than any elk Long Arrow had ever come across, the animal carried the boy all over the meadow as swiftly as the wind. Then the boy returned, jumped off his mount, and said, "Now you try it." A little timidly Long Arrow climbed up on the beautiful Elk Dog's back. Seemingly regarding him as feather-light, it took off like a flying arrow. The young man felt himself soaring through the air as a bird does, and experienced a happiness greater even than the joy he had felt when Good Running had adopted him as a grandson.

When they had finished riding the Elk Dogs, the spirit boy said to Long Arrow, "Young hunter from the land above the waters, I want you to have what you have come for. Listen to me. You may have noticed that my grandfather wears a black medicine robe as long as a woman's dress, and that he is always trying to hide his feet. Try to get a glimpse of them, for, if you do, he can refuse you nothing. He will then tell you to ask him for a gift, and you must ask for these three things: his rainbow-colored quilted belt, his black medicine robe, and a herd of these animals which you seem to like."

Long Arrow thanked him and vowed to follow his advice. For four days the young man stayed in the spirit chief's lodge, where he ate well and often went out riding on the Elk Dogs. But try as he would, he could never get a look at the old man's feet. The spirit chief always kept them carefully covered. Then on the morning of the fourth day, the old one was walking out of the tipi when his medicine robe caught in the entrance flap. As the robe opened, Long Arrow caught a glimpse of a leg and one foot. He was awed to see that it was not a human limb at all, but the glossy leg and firm hoof of an Elk Dog! He could not stifle a cry of surprise, and the old man looked over his shoulder and saw that his leg and hoof were exposed. The chief seemed a little embarrassed, but shrugged and said, "I tried to hide this, but you must have been fated to see it. Look, both of my feet are those of an Elk Dog. You may as well ask me for a gift. Don't be timid; tell me what you want."

Long Arrow spoke boldly: "I want three things: your belt of rainbow colors, your black medicine robe, and your herd of Elk Dogs."

"Well, so you're really not timid at all!" said the old man. "You ask for a lot, and I'll give it to you, except that you cannot have all my Elk Dogs; I'll give you half of them. Now I must tell you that my black medicine robe and my many-colored belt have Elk Dog magic in them. Always wear the robe when you try to catch Elk Dogs; then they can't get away from you. On quiet nights, if you listen closely to the belt, you will hear the Elk Dog dance song and Elk Dog prayers. You must learn them. And I will give you one more magic gift: this long rope woven from the hair of a white buffalo bull. With it you will never fail to catch whichever Elk Dog you want."

The spirit chief presented him with the gifts and said, "Now you must leave. At first the Elk Dogs will not follow you. Keep the medicine robe and the magic belt on at all times, and walk for four days toward the north. Never look back—always look to the north. On the fourth day the Elk Dogs will come up beside you on the left. Still don't look back. But after they have overtaken you, catch one with the rope of white buffalo hair and ride him home. Don't lose the black robe, or you will lose the Elk Dogs and never catch them again."

Long Arrow listened carefully so that he would remember. Then the old spirit chief had his wife make up a big pack of food, almost too heavy for Long Arrow to carry, and the young man took leave of his generous spirit host. The mysterious boy once again turned himself into a kingfisher and led Long Arrow to the surface of the lake, where his faithful dog greeted him joyfully. Long Arrow fed the dog, put his pack of food on the dog sled, and started walking north.

On the fourth day the Elk Dogs came up on his left side, as the spirit chief had foretold. Long Arrow snared the black one with the arched neck to ride, and he caught another to carry the pack of food. They galloped swiftly on, the dog barking at the big Elk Dogs' heels.

When Long Arrow arrived at last in his village, the people were afraid and hid. They did not recognize him astride his beautiful Elk Dog but took him for a monster, half man and half animal. Long Arrow kept calling, "Grandfather Good Running, it's your grandson. I've come back, bringing Elk Dogs!"

Recognizing the voice, Good Running came out of hiding and wept for joy, because he had given Long Arrow up for lost. Then all the others emerged from their hiding places to admire the wonderful new animals.

Long Arrow said, "My grandfather and grandmother who adopted me, I can never repay you for your kindness. Accept these wonderful Elk Dogs as my gift. Now we no longer need to be humble foot-sloggers, because these animals will carry us swiftly everywhere we want to go. Now buffalo hunting will be easy. Now our tipis will be larger, our possessions will be greater, because an Elk Dog sled can carry a load ten times bigger than that of a dog. Take them, my grandparents. I shall keep for myself only this black male and this black female, which will grow into a fine herd."

"You have indeed done something great, grandson," said Good Running, and he spoke true. The people became the bold riders of the Plains and soon could hardly imagine how they had existed without these wonderful animals.

After some time Good Running, rich and honored by all, said to Long Arrow, "Grandson, lead us to the Great Mystery Lake so we can camp by its shores. Let's visit the spirit chief and the

wondrous boy; maybe they will give us more of their power and magic gifts."

Long Arrow led the people southward and again found the Great Mystery Lake. But the waters would no longer part for him, nor would any of the kingfishers they saw turn into a boy. Nor, gazing down into the crystal-clear water, could they discover people, Elk Dogs, or a tipi. There was nothing in the lake but a few fish.

The Golem
A Jewish Legend

CZECHOSLOVAKIA

There are always mindless, dull, repetitive jobs to be done in the course of each day. For those who are blessed with the gift of intelligence, the more wearisome those dull and repetitive tasks seem. It was so for the rabbi, Judah Loew ben Bezabel, who, when faced yet again with the daily task of cleaning and bell-ringing, winding of clocks and checking of candles, mending of vestments and sweeping of steps, believed that no man (or even woman) should waste his God-given life repeating these endless tasks. And so it was that Judah Loew ben Bezabel built a creature—without mind, without soul, with little shape and no family—to do all of the tedious tasks that were his within the Prague synagogue. He called this creature the Golem, which means "lifeless lump of earth." Under the Golem's tongue he put a tablet, and the tablet allowed its limbs to move, and its shapeless body to heave itself about.

The Golem was hideous to look at, but who would see it in the shadows? It went about its work in the gloominess of the unlit synagogue only when there was no rabbi or worshipper present.

It pulled the candle stubs from the sconces and fetched new ones, it polished the brass and swept the floor, it muttered meaningless words from no living language as it sewed vestments, washed the windows and scared cats off the front steps.

Judah had written the word he loved best on the creature's forehead: AMETH, which means "truth." Perhaps he should have written GOLEM. It was so that one day old Mordecai, the town's grocer, accidentally caught sight of the creature scrubbing amid the shadows of the synagogue and he gave one terrified cry, "Oh! Death has come for me!"

Judah came running when he heard the grocer's cry and when he saw it was only the Golem, he laughed and sent it away. "That's not death, dear Mordecai. That's only my Golem," he said.

"But he has 'Death' written upon his forehead!"

"No, no. Not METH, but AMETH," said Judah, and smiled at the mistake. "The 'A' was hidden in the shadows, you see?"

And so the years went by and the Golem went about his daily tasks in a world of stone and brass and wood. Sometimes he would hear singing and he liked that. Sometimes the sun shone through the colored glass of the synagogue and splashed over the

Golem like a shower of gems. Each night the last face he would see would be Rabbi Judah's, bending low over his own, his fingers reaching into the Golem's mouth to remove the tablet. Then darkness would close over him like a coffin lid.

But one day, Judah Loew ben Bezabel forgot to remove the tablet. He was a man blessed with intelligence and such ordinary tasks tended to slip easily from his mind. The Golem moved on around the empty hall of the synagogue, though all of his tasks were completed. He checked the sconces but they were filled with new candles, he checked the steps, but there were no cats. The night stretched ahead of him like a dark corridor, so, naturally, he began to sweep it.

The broom wore down to a stump, and still the Golem continued sweeping. Then dawn rose in the town, and the sun shone full in the Golem's face for the very first time.

He went mad with joy.

It was the ferocious joy of the Earth as it shakes down trees and houses. It was the destructive joy of a child who knows no better than to break things. When people left their houses and saw the Golem roaming about, they screamed, "A monster! A ghoul!" and the Golem did not like that. He hurled the people through windows, and he loved the sound of the glass as it shattered. He hurled carts into the river, for the glory of the splash. The tablet under his tongue gave him more strength than ever before, and his simple mind teemed with new thoughts. He must taste more of this brilliant new world!

But as he continued on his way the bright light hurt his eyes, the screams of the people hurt his ears, and he could not find his master anywhere. People were throwing things at him now, and they fired loud guns. The Golem began to feel pain, as well as fright and rage. He tore at the walls of buildings, looking for Judah. He climbed church spires and threw down clocks and gargoyles. Though they tried to kill him, no one could, for he was never truly alive—only a lump of clay.

But God made Man out of a lump of clay, and Judah had made something very similar.

When the statues did not speak to him, the Golem pushed them down. The colorful market stalls intrigued him, and he snatched at the colorful awnings. The army came to meet him, so he shooed the soldiers from him, like cats from the synagogue's steps.

But where was Judah? The cacophany of a city in panic maddened the Golem, and he ripped through doors and punched down fences, looking for his master, calling for him in the shapeless language no one understood.

The Golem was hurt. He was lost. By the time Judah Loew ben Bezabel came running, his robes flapping against his legs, his face aghast at the destruction, the Golem blamed *him* for the turmoil of his mind. He turned from tearing up horse-troughs, and turned on Judah with a horrible snarl. His shapeless hands closed round the rabbi's throat, and they both fell to the ground.

Judah, half-throttled, saw the world sink to near darkness around him. His strength was nothing compared with the Golem's; he knew he could not fight. With his last conscious thought, he reached up and struck the Golem's forehead—smudging out the letter "A" from the word *ameth*, leaving only the word *meth* : death.

The Golem's eyes flew open; they flashed brightly. *"Life, not Death!"* he said quite clearly, then fell forward with the weight of an ox on top of Rabbi Judah.

One last thing you ought know: the Golem was actually quite small. Only waist-high to an average man. You can see for yourself. What remains of the Golem stands in a glass case in the Prague Museum, a clay figurine that is as ugly as sin, the Hebrew word for "Death" still scrawled upon his forehead.

The History of Jack and the Giants

ENGLAND

THE FIRST PART

In the Reign of King Arthur, near the Lands End of England, namely, the County of Cornwall, there lived a wealthy farmer, who had one only son, commonly known by the name of Jack the Giant-Killer. He was brisk, and of a lively ready wit, so that whatever he could not perform by force and strength, he completed by ingenious wit and policy. Never was any person heard of that could worst him; nay, he baffled the very learned many times by his cunning and sharp, ready inventions. For instance, when he was no more than seven years of age, his father, the farmer, sent him into the field to look after the oxen, which were then feeding in a pleasant pasture. A country vicar, by chance one day coming across the fields, called to Jack, and asked him several questions; in particular, "How many Commandments are there?" Jack told him, "There are nine." The Parson replied, "There are ten." "Nay," quoted Jack, "Mr. Parson, you are wrong; it's true there were ten, but you broke one with your maid Margery." The Parson replied, "Thou art an arch wag, Jack." "Well, Mr. Parson," said Jack, "You have asked me one question, and I have answered it, I beseech you let me ask you another. Who made these oxen?" The Parson replied, "God made them, child." "Now you are wrong again," said Jack, "for God made those bulls, but my Father and his man Hobson made oxen of them." These were the witty answers of Jack. The Parson, finding himself outwitted, trudged away, leaving Jack in a fit of laughter.

In those days the Mount of Cornwall was kept by a huge and monstrous Giant, eighteen feet in height, and about three yards in compass, of a fierce and grim countenance, the terror of all the neighboring towns and villages. His habitation was a cave in the midst of the mountain. Never would he suffer any living creature to live near him. He stole other men's cattle, which often became his prey; for whensoever he wanted food, he would wade over the main land, where he would take whatsoever he found; for the people at his approach would forsake their habitations, then he would seize upon their cows and oxen, which he would carry on his back half a dozen at a time; and as for their sheep and hogs, he would tie them round his waist like a belt. For many years he had practiced stealing cows, oxen, sheep and hogs, so that much of the county of Cornwall was impoverished by him.

But one day Jack, coming to the Town Hall when the magistrates were sitting in consultation about this Giant, asked them, "What reward they would give to any person who would destroy him?" They replied, "He should have all the Giant's treasure in recompense." Said Jack, "Then I myself will undertake the work."

Jack, having undertaken the task, furnished himself with a horn, shovel and pick-ax, and went over to the Mount in the beginning of a dark winter evening. He fell to work, and before morning had dug a pit two and twenty feet deep, and almost as broad, covering the pit over with long sticks and straw; then strewing a little of the mold upon it, it appeared like the plain ground. This done, Jack placed himself on the contrary side of the pit. Just as day dawned, he put his horn to his mouth, and blew "Tan-tive, Tan-tive," which roused the Giant, who came running toward Jack, saying: "You incorrigible villain, have you come here to disturb my rest? You shall pay dearly for this. Satisfaction I will have, and it shall be this, I will have you whole, and broil you for my breakfast." These words were no sooner out of his mouth, but he tumbled headlong into the pit, his heavy fall making the very foundation of the Mount shake. "O Giant," said Jack, "where are you now? In faith you are fallen into Lob's Pound, where I will plague you for your threatening words. What do you think now of broiling me for your breakfast? Will no other diet serve you but poor Jack?" Thus having tantalized the Giant for a while, he gave him such a considerable blow upon the crown of his head with his pick-ax that he tumbled down and, with a dreadful groan, died. This done, Jack threw the earth in upon him, and so buried him. And then going and searching his cave, he found much treasure. Now when the magistrates who employed him heard the work was over, they sent for him, declaring that he should henceforth be called Jack the Giant-Killer, and in honor thereto, presented him with a sword, together with an embroidered belt, on which these words were wrought in letters of gold:

Here's the right valiant Cornish Man,
Who slew the Giant Cormilan.

The news of Jack's victory was soon spread over the western parts, so that another Giant named Blunderboar, hearing of it, vowed to be revenged on Jack, if it ever was his fortune to see him. This Giant kept an enchanted castle, situated in the midst of a lonesome wood. Now Jack, about four months later, walking by the borders of the same place, in his journey toward Wales, grew weary, and therefore sat himself down by the side of a pleasant fountain, where a deep sleep suddenly seized him; at which time the Giant coming there for water found him, and by the lines written upon his belt knew him to be Jack, who killed his Brother Giant; and therefore without making any words, he snatched him upon his shoulder to carry him home to his enchanted castle. Now as they passed through a thicket, the rustling of the boughs awakened Jack, who finding himself in the clutches of the Giant, was strangely surprised, but it was only the beginning of his terror; for entering within the first walls of his castle, he beheld the ground covered with bones and skulls of dead men; the Giant telling Jack that his bones would enlarge the number of what he sees there.

This said, he brought him into a large parlor, where Jack beheld the bloody quarters of some that were lately slain.

And in the next room were hearts and livers. The Giant, to terrify Jack, told him that men's hearts were the choicest of his diet, for he commonly, as he said, ate them with pepper and vinegar, adding that he did not question but that Jack's heart would make him a dainty bit. This said, he locked poor Jack into an upper room, leaving him there while he went to fetch another

Giant, living in the same wood, that he might partake of the pleasure that they should have in the destruction of poor Jack. Now while he was gone, dreadful shrieks and cries affrighted poor Jack, especially a voice that continually cried,

> *"Do what you can to get away,*
> *Or you'll become the Giant's prey;*
> *He's gone to fetch his Brother, who*
> *Will kill, and likewise torture you."*

This dreadful noise so amazed poor Jack that he was ready to run distracted, then going to a window he opened a casement where he beheld afar off the two Giants coming together. "Now," said Jack to himself, "my death or deliverance is at hand." There were strong cords in the room by him, of which he made two, at the ends of which he made a noose, and while the Giant was unlocking the iron gate he threw the ropes over their heads, and drew the other end across a beam, which he pulled with all his main strength, till he had throttled them. Then, fastening the ropes to the beam, he returned to the window, where he beheld the two Giants black in the face. Sliding down by the rope, he came to their heads, where the helpless Giants could not defend themselves, and drawing out his sword, slew them both, and delivered himself from their intended cruelty. Taking the keys, he entered the castle, where, upon strict search, he found three fair ladies, tied by the hair of their heads, almost starved to death, who told Jack that their husbands had been slain by the Giant, and they were kept many days without food, in order to feed upon the flesh of their murdered husbands, which they would not, so they were to starve to death. "Sweet ladies," said Jack, "I have destroyed the Monster, with his brutish brother, by which I obtained your liberties." This said, he presented them with the keys of the castle, and so proceeded on his journey to Wales.

Jack having but little money, thought it prudent to make the best of his way by traveling hard, and at length losing his road was delayed, and could not get a place of entertainment, till coming to a valley between two hills, he found a large house in that lonesome place, and by reason of his present necessity, he took courage to knock at the gate, where to his amazement, there came forth a monstrous Giant with two heads. Yet he did not seem to be so fiery as the others had been, for he was a Welsh Giant, and what he did was by private and secret malice, under the false show of friendship; for when Jack told his condition he bid him welcome, showing him a room with a bed in it, where he might take his

night's repose, whereupon Jack undressed, and as the Giant was walking away to another apartment, Jack heard him mutter these words to himself,

"Tho' here you lodge with me this night,
You shall not see the morning light,
My club shall dash your brains out quite."

"So you say," said Jack, "that's like one of your Welsh tricks, yet I hope to be cunning enough for you." Then getting out of his bed and feeling about in the dark, he found a thick billet, which he laid in the bed in his stead, and laid himself in a dark corner of the room. In the dead of the night came the Welsh Giant with his club, and struck several heavy blows upon his bed, where Jack had laid the billet, and then returned to his chamber, supposing he had broken all the bones in his skin.

The next morning Jack came to give him thanks for his lodging. Said the Giant, "How have you rested? Did you not feel something in the night?" "No, nothing," said Jack, "but a rat, which gave me three or four slaps with her tail."

Soon after the Giant arose, he went to his breakfast, which was a bowl of hasty-pudding containing four gallons, and gave Jack the like quantity. Jack was loathe to let the Giant know he could not eat the same, so he got a large leather bag, and put it under his loose coat. He then secretly conveyed the pudding into it, telling the Giant he would show him a trick. Then, taking a large knife, he ripped open the bag, which the Giant supposed to be his belly, and out came the hasty-pudding, which the Giant, seeing, cried out, "Cotsplut, hur can do that Trick hurself!" Then taking a sharp knife he ripped open his own belly from the bottom to the top, and out dropped his tripes and trolly-bubs, so that he fell down dead. Thus Jack outwitted the Welsh Giant, and proceeded forward on his journey.

King Arthur's son desired of his Father to furnish him with a certain sum of money, that he might go seek his fortune in the principality of Wales, where a beautiful lady lived, whom he heard was possessed with seven evil spirits; the King, his Father, counselled him against it, yet he would not be persuaded from it, so that he granted what he requested, which was one horse loaded with money, with another for himself to ride on.

Thus he went forth without any attendance, and after several days travel he came to a market town in Wales, where he beheld a vast concourse of people gathered together. The King's son demanded the reason of it, and was told that they had arrested a corpse for many large sums of money, which the deceased owed when he died. The King's son replied, "It is pity that creditors should be so cruel. Go bury the dead," said he, "and let his creditors come to my lodging, and their debts shall be discharged."

Accordingly they came, and in such great numbers, that before night he had almost left himself penniless. Now Jack the Giant-Killer being there, and seeing the generosity of the King's son, was highly taken with him, and desired to be his servant. It was agreed upon, and the next morning they set forward; when riding out at the town's end, an old woman called after him, crying out, "He has owed me two pence this seven years, pray sir, pay me as well as the rest." He put his hand in his pocket and gave it her, it being the last he had left.

Then the King's son, turning to Jack, said, "I cannot tell how to subsist in my intended journey." "For that," said Jack, "take you no thought nor care, let me alone, we will not want." Now Jack had a small coin in his pocket, and at noon it served to give them a refreshment, after which they had not a penny left between them. The afternoon they spent in travel and familiar discourse, till the sun began to grow low, at which time the King's son said, "Jack, since we have no money, where can we think to lodge this night?" Jack replied, "Master, we will do well enough, for I have an uncle who lives within two miles of this place; he is a huge and monstrous giant with three heads, he'll fight five hundred men in armor, and make them flee before him."

"Alas!" said the King's son, "what should we do there? He'll certainly chop us up in a mouthful, though we are scarcely enough to fill one of his hollow teeth."

"It is no matter for that," said Jack, "I myself will go before and prepare the way for you, therefore tarry and wait my return."

He waited, and Jack rode full speed, when coming to the gate of the castle, he knocked with that force that made the neighboring hills resound.

The Giant, with a voice like thunder, roared out, "Who is there?" He was answered, "None but your poor cousin Jack." Said he, "What news with my poor cousin Jack?" He replied, "Dear uncle, heavy news this is." "Prithee what heavy news can come to me? I am a Giant, with three heads, and besides, thou knowest I can fight five hundred men in armor, and make them fly like chaff before the wind." "O, but," said Jack, "here is the King's son coming with a thousand men in armor to kill you, and destroy all that you have." "O cousin Jack, that is heavy news indeed; I have a large vault under ground, where I will immediately run and hide myself, and thou shalt lock, bolt, and bar me in, and keep the keys till the King's son is gone."

Now Jack having secured the Giant, he returned and fetched his master, and were both heartily merry with wine, and of the dainties which the house afforded. That night they rested in pleasant lodgings, while the poor Giant lay trembling in a vault under the ground.

In the morning Jack furnished his master with a fresh supply of gold and silver, and then set him three miles forward of his journey, concluding he was then pretty well out of the smell of the Giant, and then returned and let his uncle out of his hole, who asked Jack what he should give him for his care, in regard to see his castle was not demolished. "Why," said Jack, "I desire nothing but the old rusty sword, coat, and slippers, which are at your bed's head." Said the Giant, "Thou shalt have them, and prithee keep them for my sake, for they are things of excellent use. The coat will keep you invisible, the cap will furnish you with knowledge, the sword will cut in sunder whatever you strike, the shoes are of extraordinary swiftness; they may be serviceable to you, and therefore take them with all my heart." Jack took them, and so followed his master.

Jack having overtaken his master, they soon arrived at the lady's house, and finding the King's son to be a suitor, prepared a banquet for him, which being ended, she wiped his mouth with a handkerchief, saying, "You must show me this handkerchief tomorrow morning, or else lose your head." And with that put it into her bosom.

The King's son went to bed right sorrowful, but Jack's cap of knowledge instructed him how to obtain it. In the middle of the night the Princess called upon her chariot to carry her to the Devil. Jack put on his coat of darkness, and with his shoes of swiftness, was there before her, and by reason of his coat, they could not see him.

When she entered the Devil's lair, she gave him the handkerchief. He laid it upon a shelf, from whence Jack took it and brought it to his master, who, showing it to the lady the next day, saved his life.

The next night she saluted the young Prince, telling him he must show her the lips tomorrow morning that she kissed last this night, or lose his head. He replied, "If you kissed none but mine, I will." "Tis neither here nor there," said she, "if you do not, death is your portion."

At midnight she went as before, and was angry with the Devil for letting the handkerchief go. "But now," said she, "I shall be too hard for the young Prince, for I will kiss thy lips," which she did.

Jack standing by, with his sword of sharpness, cut off the Devil's head, and brought it under his invisible coat to his master, who laid it at the end of his bolster, and in the morning when the Princess came up, he pulled it out by the horns, and showed her the Devil's lips, which she had kissed last.

Thus having answered her twice, the enchantment broke, and the evil spirit left her, at which time she appeared in all her beauty, a sweet and virtuous creature.

They were married the next morning, and soon after returned with joy to the court of King Arthur, when Jack for his good service was made one of the Knights of the Round Table.

THE SECOND PART OF THE HISTORY
OF JACK AND THE GIANTS

Jack, having been successful in all his undertakings, and resolving not to be idle in the future, but to perform what service he could for the honor of his King and country, humbly requested the King, his master, to fit him forth with a horse and money to travel in search of strange and new adventures. "For," said he, "there are many Giants yet living in the remote parts of this kingdom, and the dominion of Wales, to the unspeakeable damage of your majesty's liege subjects; wherefore, may it please you to give me encouragement, and I will in a short time cut them off root and branch, and so rid the realm of those cruel Giants and devouring monsters in nature." Now, when the King had heard his noble propositions, and had duly considered the mischievous practices of those blood-thirsty Giants, he immediately granted what honest Jack requested; and, on the first day of March, being thoroughly furnished with all necessaries for his progress, he took his leave, not only of King Arthur, but likewise of all the trusty and hardy knights belonging to the Round Table, who after much satisfaction and friendly greeting, parted; the King and nobles to their country palace, and Jack the Giant-Killer to the eager pursuit of fortune's favor; taking with him the cap of knowledge, sword of sharpness, shoes of swiftness, and likewise the invisible coat, the better to perfect and complete the dangerous enterprises that lay before him.

Jack traveled over vast hills and mountains, when at the end of three days he came to a large and spacious wood, through which he must need pass; where, all of a sudden, to his amazement, he heard dreadful shrieks and cries; whereupon, casting his eyes around, to observe what it might be, beheld a Giant, with a worthy knight and his lady, whom he held by the hair of their heads in his hands, with as much ease, as if they had been but a pair of gloves; the sight of which melted honest Jack in tears of pity and compassion. Alighting from his horse, which he left tied to an oak tree, and then putting on his invisible coat, under which he carried his infallible sword, Jack came up to the Giant, and tho' he made several passes at him, yet nevertheless he could not reach the trunk of his body, by reason of his height, tho' he wounded his thighs in several places; but at length, giving him with both hands a swinging stroke, cut off both his legs, just below the knee, so that the trunk of his body caused not only the ground to shake, but likewise the trees to tremble with the force of his fall; at which, by mere fortune, the knight and his fair lady escaped his rage. Then Jack had time to talk with him, setting his foot on his neck, saying, "Thou savage and barbarous wretch, I am come to execute upon you the just reward of your villainy." And with that, running him through and through, the monster sent forth a hideous groan; and so yielded up his life into the hands of the valiant conqueror Jack the Giant-Killer, while the noble knight and virtuous lady were both joyful spectators of his sudden downfall, and their own deliverance. This being done, the courteous knight and his fair lady not only returned him hearty thanks for their deliverance, but also invited him home, there to refresh himself after the dreadful encounter, as likewise to receive some reward by way of gratitude for his good service. "I cannot," says Jack, "be at ease till I find out the den that was this monster's habitation." The knight, hearing this, waxed right sorrowful, and replied, "Noble stranger, it is too much to run a second hazard. For, note, this monster lived in a den under yonder mountain, with a brother of his, more fierce than himself; and, therefore, if you should go thither, and perish in the attempt, it would be heart-breaking both for me and my lady; therefore, let me persuade you to go with us, and desist from any further pursuit." "Nay," said Jack, "if there be another, say; were there twenty, I would shed the last drop of blood in my body before one of them should escape my fury; and when I have finished this task, I will come and pay my respects to you." So taking direction to their habitation, he mounted his horse, leaving them to return home, while he went in pursuit of the deceased Giant's brother.

Jack had not rid past a mile and a half before he came in sight of the cave's mouth, near to the entrance of which he beheld this other Giant, sitting upon a huge block of timber, with a knotted iron club lying by his side, waiting (as he supposed) for his brother's return with his barbarous prey, his goggling eyes appearing like terrible flames of fire; his countenance grim and ugly, for his cheeks appeared like a couple of large flitches of bacon; moreover, the bristles of his beard seemed to resemble rods of iron-wire; his locks hung down upon his brawny broad shoulders like curled snakes or hissing adders. Jack alighted from his horse, and put him into a thicket, then with his coat of darkness he approached something nearer to behold this figure, and said softly, "O! Are you there? It will not be long before I take you by the beard." The Giant all this while could not see him, by reason of his invisible coat; so that coming up close to him, valiant Jack aimed a blow at his head with his sword of sharpness (and missing something of his aim), cut off the Giant's nose, whose nostrils were wider than a pair of Jack-boots. The pain was terrible, and so he put up his hands to feel for his nose, and when he could not find it, he raved and roared louder than claps of

thunder; and though he turned up his glaring eyes, he could not see from whence the blow came, which had done him that great unkindness; yet nevertheless, he took up his iron-knotted club and began to lay about him like one that was stark staring mad. "Nay," said Jack, "if you are for that sport, then I will dispatch you quickly, for fear an accidental blow will fall." Then, as the Giant rose from his block, Jack made no more fuss, but ran his sword up to the hilt in the Giant's fundament, where he left it sticking for a while, and stood himself laughing (with his hands akimbo) to see the Giant caper and dance the canaries, with the sword in his backside, crying out, he should die, he should die, with the griping of the guts. Thus did the Giant continue raving for an hour or more, and at length fell down dead, whose dreadful fall almost crushed poor Jack, had he not been nimble to avoid the same. This being done, Jack cut off both the Giants' heads, and sent them to King Arthur by a wagoner that he hired for the same purpose; together with an account of his prosperous success in all his undertakings.

Jack, having thus dispatched these two monsters, resolved to enter the cave in search of the Giants' treasure. He passed along through many turnings and windings, which led him at length to a room paved with free-stone, at the upper end of which was a boiling cauldron; and on the right side stood a large table, where he supposed the Giants used to dine. Then he came to an iron gate, where there was a window secured with bars of iron, through which he looked, and there beheld a vast many miserable captives; who, seeing Jack at a distance, cried out with a loud voice, "Alas! Young man, art thou come to be one among us in this miserable den?" "Aye," said Jack, "I hope I shall not tarry long here: but, pray tell me, what's the meaning of your captivity?" "Why," said one young man, "I'll tell you. We are persons that have been taken by the Giants that kept this cave, and here are kept till such time as they have occasion for a feast more than ordinary, and then the fattest among us is slaughtered, and prepared for their devouring jaws; it is not long since they took three for the same purpose; nay, many are the times they have dined on murdered men." "Say you so," said Jack. "Well, I have given them both such a dinner, that it will be long enough before they'll have occasion for any more." The miserable captives were amazed at his words. "You may believe me," said Jack, "for I have slain them with the point of my sword; and, as for their monstrous heads, I sent them in a wagon to the court of King Arthur, as trophies of my unparalleled victories."

"And, as testimony of the truth," he said, and he unlocked the iron gate setting the miserable captives at liberty; who all rejoiced like condemned malefactors, at the sight of a reprieve. Then, leading them all together to the aforesaid room, he placed them round the table, and set before them two quarters of beef, also bread and wine, so that he feasted them very plentifully. Supper being ended, they searched the Giant's coffers, where finding a vast store of gold and silver, Jack equally divided it amongst them; they all returned him hearty thanks for their treasure, and miraculous deliverance. That night they went to their rest, and in the morning they arose, and departed; the captives to their respective towns, and places of abode; and Jack to the knight's house, whom he had formerly delivered from the hands of the Giants.

It was about sunrise when Jack mounted his horse to proceed on his journey; and by the help of his directions he came to the knight's house something before noon, where he was received with all demonstrations of joy imaginable by the knight and his lady; who, in honorable respect to Jack, prepared a feast, which lasted many days, inviting all the gentry in the adjacent parts; to whom the worthy knight was pleased to relate the manner of his former danger, and miraculous deliverance by the undaunted courage of Jack the Giant-Killer; and, by way of gratitude, he presented him with a ring of gold, on which was engraved by curious art, the picture of the Giant, dragging a distressed knight and his fair lady by the hair of the head; with this motto:

We are in sad distress you see,
Under a Giant's fierce command;
But gain'd our lives and liberty,
By valiant Jack's victorious hand.

Now, among the vast assembly then present, were five aged gentlemen, who were fathers to some of those miserable captives that Jack had lately set at liberty; who, understanding that he was the person that had performed such miraculous wonders, they immediately paid their venerable respects. After which, their mirth increased, and the smiling bowls went freely round, to the prosperous success of the victorious conqueror. But, in the midst of all this mirth, a dark cloud appeared, which daunted the hearts of this honorable assembly, and company. Thus it was; a messenger came, and brought the dismal tidings of the approach of one Thunderdel, a huge Giant with two heads; who, having heard of the death of his two kinsmen, the two Giants aforesaid, came from Northern Wales in search of Jack; to be revenged of him, for their miserable downfall, and was within a mile of the knight's house, the country people flying before him from their houses and habitations, like chaff before the wind. When they had related this, Jack, not a whit daunted, said, "Let him come. I am prepared with a tool to pick his teeth; and you, gentlemen and ladies, walk but forth into the garden and you shall be the joyful spectators of this monstrous Giant's death and destruction." To which they consented, everyone wishing him good fortune in this dangerous enterprise.

The situation of the Knight's house was as follows: it was placed in the midst of a small island, surrounded by a vast moat, thirty feet deep and twenty feet wide, over which lay a drawbridge, whereof Jack employed two men to cut it on both sides, almost to the middle, and then dressing himself in his coat of darkness, likewise putting on his shoes of swiftness, he marched forth against the Giant, with his sword of sharpness ready drawn; yet, when he came close up to him, the Giant could not see Jack, by reason of his invisible coat, which he had on, yet nevertheless he was aware of some approaching danger, which made him cry out in these following words:

> *"Fe, fi, fo, fum,*
> *I smell the blood of an* English *man,*
> *Be he alive, or be he dead,*
> *I'll grind his bones to make my bread."*

"Is that so?" said Jack, "then thou art a monstrous miller indeed; but how, if I should serve thee as I did the two Giants of late? In my conscience I should spoil your practice for the future." At which time the Giant spoke out with a voice like roaring thunder: "Art thou that villain that destroyed my two kinsmen? Then I will tear thee with my teeth, suck thy blood, and what is more, I'll grind thy bones to powder." "You must catch me first," said Jack; and with that threw off his coat of darkness that the Giant might see him clearly; and then run from him, as if through fear. The Giant, with foaming mouth and glaring eyes, followed after, like a walking castle, making the foundation of the earth, as it were, shake at every step. Jack led him in a dance three or four times round the moat belonging to the knight's house, that the gentlemen and ladies might take a full view of this huge monster in nature, who followed Jack with all his might, but could not overtake him by reason of Jack's shoes of swiftness, which carried him faster than the Giant could follow. At length, Jack, to finish the work, took over the bridge, the Giant pursuing him with his iron club upon his shoulder; but, coming to the middle of the drawbridge, that, with the weight of his body, and the dreadful steps that he took, broke down, and he tumbled head first into the water, where he roared and wallowed like a whale. Jack, standing upon the side of the wharf, laughed at the Giant, and said, "You would grind my bones to powder; here you have water enough, pray, where is your mill?" The Giant fretted and fumed to hear Jack scoff at that rate; and, though he plunged from place to place in the moat, yet he could not get out to be revenged on his adversary. Jack at length got a cart rope and cast it over the Giant's two heads, and with a slip knot and by the help of a team of horses, dragged him out again, with which he was near strangled. Before he would let him loose, he cut off both his heads with his sword of sharpness, in the full view of all the worthy assembly of knights, gentlemen and ladies, who gave a joyful shout when they saw the Giant fairly dispatched. Then, before he would either eat or drink, he sent the heads one after the other to the court of King Arthur; which being done, Jack, with the ladies, returned to their mirth and pastime, which lasted for many days.

After some time spent in triumph, mirth and pastime, Jack grew weary of riotous living, wherefore taking his leave of the knights and ladies, he set forward in search of new adventures. Through many woods and groves he passed, meeting with nothing remarkable, till at length coming near the foot of a high mountain, late at night, he knocked at the door of a lonesome house, at which time an ancient man, with a head as white as snow, arose and let him in. "Father," said Jack, "have you any entertainment for a benighted traveler that has lost his way?" "Yes," said the old man, "if you will accept of such commendations as my poor cottage will afford, thou shalt be right welcome." Jack returned him many thanks for his civility, and down they sat together, and the old man began to discourse to him as follows. "Son," said he, "I am aware that thou art the great conqueror of Giants, and it lies in thy power to free this part of the country

from an intolerable burden which we groan under; for, behold, my son, on the top of this high mountain, there is an enchanted castle, kept by a huge and monstrous Giant named Galigantus; who, by the help of an old conjuror, betrays many knights and ladies into his strong castle; where by magic art, they are transformed into sundry shapes and forms. But above all I lament the miserable misfortune of a duke's daughter, whom they fetched from her father's garden by magic art, and brought her through the air in a mourning chariot, drawn as it were by two fiery dragons, and having secured her within the walls of the castle, she was immediately transformed into the shape of a white hind, where she miserably mourned her misfortune. And though many worthy knights have endeavoured to break the enchantment, and work her deliverance, none of them could accomplish this great work by reason of two dreadful Griffins, who are fixed by magic art at the entrance of the castle gate, and who destroyed the knights at the first approach, so soon as they had fixed their eyes upon them. But you, my son, being furnished with an invisible coat, may pass by them undiscovered; where on the brazen gates of the castle, you shall find it engraved in large characters, by what means the enchantment may be broken." The old man having ended his discourse, Jack gave him his hand, with a faithful promise, that in the morning he would venture his life for the breaking of the enchantment, and freeing the lady, together with the others that were miserable partners in her calamity.

Having refreshed themselves with a small morsel of meat, they lay down to rest; and in the morning Jack arose, and put on his invisible coat, cap of knowledge, and shoes of swiftness, and so prepared himself for the dangerous enterprise. Now, when he had ascended to the top of the mountain, he discovered the two fiery Griffins. He passed on between them without any fear, for they could not see him by reason of his invisible coat. Now, when he was beyond them, he cast his eyes around, where he found upon the gates a golden trumpet, hung in a chain of fine silver, under which these lines were engraved:

Whoever shall this trumpet blow,
Shall soon the Giant overthrow;
And break the black enchantment straight,
So shall all be in happy state.

Jack had no sooner read this inscription then he blew the trumpet, at which time the vast foundation of the castle trembled,

and the Giant, together with the conjuror, was in a horrid confusion, biting their thumbs, and tearing their hair, knowing their wicked reign was at an end; at which time Jack, standing at the Giant's elbow, as he was stooping to take up his club, at one blow with his sword of sharpness, cut off his head. The conjuror, seeing this, mounted immediately in the air, and was carried away in a whirlwind. Thus was the whole enchantment broken, and every knight and lady, that had been for a long time transformed into birds and beasts, returned to their proper shapes and likenesses again; and as for the castle, though it seemed at first to be a vast place of strength and bigness, it vanished away like a cloud of smoke; whereupon a universal joy appeared amongst the released knights and ladies. This being done, the head of Galigantus was likewise, according to his accustomed manner, conveyed to the court of King Arthur, as a present to the King.

The very next day, having refreshed the knights and ladies at the old man's habitation, who lived at the foot of the mountain, Jack set forward for the court of King Arthur, with those knights and ladies that he had so honorably delivered. When coming to the King and having related all the passages of his fierce encounters, Jack's fame rung through the whole court, and as a reward of his good service, the King prevailed with the aforesaid duke to bestow his daughter in marriage on honest Jack, protesting that there was no man living so worthy of her as he; all which the duke very honorably consented to. So married they were, and not only the court, but likewise the kingdom, was filled with joy and triumph at the wedding. After which the King (as a reward for all his good services done for his nation) bestowed upon him a noble habitation, with a very plentiful estate thereunto belonging, where Jack and his lady lived the rest of their days in great joy and happiness.

How Kwaku Ananse Was Punished for His Bad Manners

GHANA

O ne year there had been no rain in the forest and everything was so dry that there was no food in Ananse's village. He and his family went hungry; they searched in vain for something to eat.

Now Ananse's son, Ntikuma, was growing up and was able to go and hunt for himself. One day, wandering far from the village, he came upon a big hole in the ground, and there, lying near it, were three large nuts. Now Ntikuma was very hungry and, realizing that three nuts would not feed a family, he decided to eat them himself and then go on with his search for food.

He cracked the first one carefully on a stone, but it shot out of the shell and bounced into the big hole. He tried the second one, being more careful, but somehow the nut eluded him and rolled down the hole. In despair he took the third nut and swore that if he did not eat it he would go down into the hole and look for the nuts. Sure enough, when the shell split, the nut shot up into the air, over Ntikuma's shoulder and into the hole. He stood up and made for the hole.

Now the hole was dark and deep, but Ntikuma did not lack courage and, making himself a rope of creepers, he climbed down into the hole. To his surprise it became lighter at the bottom, and he climbed off the rope into another land.

An old woman was sitting nearby, eating nuts by the door of her hut. He greeted her politely.

"Why have you come here?" she asked.

"I was looking for food, Grandmother," he said. "I found three nuts but they all rolled into this hole and I came down after them."

The old woman stared at Ntikuma, saw he was telling the truth and spoke again. "Go behind the house. There is a big farm there and there are plenty of yams. Go and collect some, but the ones that say 'Take me' do not touch, only those that say 'Do not take me.' Bring me some of those and we will cook them. The others you shall take home."

Ntikuma went into the farm and did exactly as he was told. He left strictly alone the yams that asked to be taken, and waited to find those that told him to leave them alone. At last he found these and collected as many as he could carry. He brought them back to the old lady. By now she had a fire ready and, handing Ntikuma a knife, she said: "Peel off the outside carefully and put it in the pot. The inside, throw away." Ntikuma did as he was told and soon a wonderful smell came from the fire. When the meal was ready, the old lady asked Ntikuma to sit down with her and gave him a bowl of food. It was delicious. Ntikuma ate quickly as he was hungry. Then he sat back to watch the old woman. He saw that she was eating through her nose. He was far too polite to remark on this, and just sat and waited until she had finished. Then he said he must go home, and begged to take some yams to his mother. These the old lady willingly gave him, but first she told him to go into her room. There he would find two drums, one big and one small. He was to take the small one home with him. This he did, thanking the old woman warmly for her gifts. She told him that when he was hungry he had only to say "Cover" to the drum and food would come. So he went home to his family, rejoicing.

Ntikuma told the whole story to his family after they had had the first good meal for days. His father, being jealous of his son's success, said he would go the next day and bring back something even better. He chided his son for obeying so meekly the old woman who was obviously a witch and could have given him more.

Early the next day, Ananse went off to try his hand. So good were Ntikuma's directions that he easily found the spot and saw three nuts lying by the hole. "I will follow the nuts into the hole," he said. He cracked them right near the edge but instead of rolling in, they seemed determined to stay outside. In the end he had to push the last nut in. The rope Ntikuma had made was still there and he climbed down into the hole.

Sure enough, there was the old woman eating nuts. Ananse looked at her and said, "My, what an ugly old woman you are." But the old lady took no notice of him and went on eating nuts. Then she asked him why he had come to see her. "Why, to get food, of course," said Ananse. "If you can give my son much, why then you must be able to give me more."

The old lady looked at him and smiled. "If you are so sure, then go behind the house. There is a farm there and there are plenty of yams. Do not take the ones that say 'Take me' but only those that say 'Do not take me.'" Ananse replied, "I am sure you are cheating me. I shall take which I please." And he stumped off into the farm.

The first yam he saw was an enormous one. "Take me, take me," it cried. Ananse immediately went and cut it. But when he cut it open he found that it was full of hard nuts. Then he went further into the farm and finally found the yams that said "Do not take me," and collected a pile and took them back to the cottage.

The old lady had a pot boiling on the fire. She said to Ananse, "Peel the yams carefully and throw away the inside, boiling the outside." Ananse was angry. "What do you take me for?" he said. "One always cooks the inside of the yam." And he put the inside of the yam in the pot and threw away the skin. He came back and looked in the pot and saw that it was full of stones. He had thrown the skins away, so he was forced to go to the farm and collect more yams, and to the stream and collect more water for the pot. Then he did as the old woman said.

At last they sat down to their meal. Ananse stared at the old woman, seeing she was eating through her nose. "What a filthy habit," he said. "Why do you eat through your nose?" Then he laughed and laughed at the old woman. But she kept silent. Soon he pushed back his stool and said that he must go home.

The old woman watched him collect his pile of yams and then said to him, "Before you go, go into my room. You will find two drums, one big and one small. Take the small one home with you."

Ananse went into the old lady's room and saw a very beautiful big drum and a small plain one. "I am not going to take the small one," he thought. "The big one will probably give me gold as well as food." So he lifted the big one on his shoulder and, without giving another look at the old woman, climbed up the rope and went home.

It was with pride that Ananse put the big drum on the floor of his hut. He told the others to gather round and look at it. Then, fearing that they might take whatever treasure it produced, he asked them to go and fetch wood and water so that they could have a feast. Aso, his wife, and Ntikuma willingly went out to look for wood and water, wondering what wonders they would see on their return.

Kwaku Ananse sat down in front of the drum, admiring its carvings. He went to the door to make sure no one was about. Then he sat, and said in a loud voice, "Cover."

Kwaku Ananse had taken the wrong drum. As soon as he had pronounced the magic word, there was not a wonderful meal, there were no gold or treasures, but Ananse himself saw with horror that his whole body was covered with sores and scabs. He was not fit to be seen. He cried out and ran from the house. The drum, having completed its task, disappeared. The family searched and searched for Ananse, but knowing his greed they took it for granted that he had gone off to enjoy his treasure alone. After many months, he returned home, bearing for always the scars of his many sores and remaining remarkably silent about his drum.

Why the Fish Laughed

INDIA

As a certain fisherwoman passed by a palace, carrying her fish, the Queen appeared at one of the windows and beckoned her to come near and show what she had. At that moment a very big fish jumped about in the bottom of the basket.

"Is it a he or a she?" inquired the Queen. "I wish to purchase a she-fish."

On hearing this, the fish laughed aloud.

"It's a he," replied the fisherwoman, and proceeded on her rounds.

The Queen returned to her room in a great rage; and on coming to see her in the evening, the King noticed that something had disturbed her.

"Are you indisposed?" he said.

"No; but I am very much annoyed at the strange behavior of a fish. A woman brought me one today, and on my inquiring whether it was a male or female, the fish laughed most rudely."

"A fish laugh! Impossible! You must be dreaming."

"I am not a fool. I speak of what I have seen with my own eyes and have heard with my own ears."

"Passing strange! Be it so. I will inquire concerning it."

On the morrow the King repeated to his vizier what his wife had told him, and bade him investigate the matter, and be ready with a satisfactory answer within six months, on pain of death. The vizier promised to do his best, though he felt almost certain of failure. For five months he labored indefatigably to find a reason for the laughter of the fish. He sought everywhere and from everyone. The wise and learned, and they who were skilled in magic and in all manner of trickery, were consulted. Nobody, however, could explain the matter; and so he returned broken-hearted to his house, and began to arrange his affairs in prospect of certain death, for he had had sufficient experience of the King to know that his Majesty would not go back on his threat. Amongst other things, he advised his son to travel for a time, until the King's anger should have somewhat cooled.

The young fellow, who was both clever and handsome, started off whithersoever Kismet might lead him. He had been gone some days, when he fell in with an old farmer, who also was on a journey to a certain village. Finding the old man very pleasant, he asked him if he might accompany him, professing to be on a visit to the same place. The old farmer agreed, and they walked along together. The day was hot, and the way was long and weary.

"Don't you think it would be pleasanter if you and I sometimes gave each other a lift?" said the youth.

"What a fool the man is!" thought the old farmer.

Presently they passed through a field of corn ready for the sickle, and looking like a sea of gold as it waved to and fro in the breeze.

"Is this eaten or not?" said the young man.

Not understanding his meaning, the old man replied, "I don't know."

After a little while the two travelers arrived at a big village, where the young man gave his companion a clasp-knife, and said, "Take this, friend, and get two horses with it; but mind and bring it back, for it is very precious."

The old man, looking half amused and half angry, pushed back the knife, muttering something to the effect that his friend was either a fool himself or else trying to play the fool with him. The young man pretended not to notice his reply, and remained almost silent till they reached the city, a short distance outside which was the old farmer's house. They walked about the bazaar and went to the mosque, but nobody saluted them or invited them to come in and rest.

"What a large cemetery!" exclaimed the young man.

"What does the man mean," thought the old farmer, "calling this largely populated city a cemetery?"

On leaving the city their way led through a cemetery where a few people were praying beside a grave and distributing chapatis and kulchas to passersby, in the name of their beloved dead. They beckoned to the two travelers and gave them as much as they would.

"What a splendid city this is!" said the young man.

"Now, the man must surely be demented!" thought the old farmer. "I wonder what he will do next? He will be calling the land water, and the water land; and be speaking of light where there is darkness, and of darkness when it is light." However, he kept his thoughts to himself.

Presently they had to wade through a stream that ran along the edge of the cemetery. The water was rather deep, so the old farmer took off his shoes and robes and crossed over; but the young man waded through it with his shoes and robes on.

"Well! I never did see such a perfect fool, both in word and in deed," said the old man to himself.

However, he liked the fellow; and thinking that he would amuse his wife and daughter, he invited him to come and stay at his house as long as he had occasion to remain in the village.

"Thank you very much," the young man replied; "but let me first inquire, if you please, whether the beam of your house is strong."

The old farmer left him in despair, and entered his house laughing.

"There is a man in yonder field," he said, after returning their greetings. "He has come the greater part of the way with me, and I wanted him to put up here as long as he had to stay in this village. But the fellow is such a fool that I cannot make anything out of him. He wants to know if the beam of this house is all right. The man must be mad!" and saying this, he burst into a fit of laughter.

"Father," said the farmer's daughter, who was a very sharp and wise girl, "this man, whosoever he is, is no fool, as you deem him. He only wishes to know if you can afford to entertain him."

"Oh! Of course," replied the farmer. "I see. Well, perhaps you can help me to solve some of his other mysteries. While we were walking together he asked whether he should carry me or I should carry him, as he thought that would be a pleasanter mode of proceeding."

"Most assuredly," said the girl. "He meant that one of you should tell a story to beguile the time."

"Oh, yes. Well, we were passing through a cornfield when he asked me whether it was eaten or not."

"And didn't you know the meaning of this, Father? He simply wished to know if the owner of the field was in debt or not; because if the owner was in debt, then the produce of the field was as good as eaten to him; that is, it would have to go to his creditors."

"Yes, yes, yes, of course! Then, on entering a certain village, he bade me take his clasp-knife and get two horses with it, and bring back the knife again to him."

"Are not two stout sticks as good as two horses for helping one along on the road? He only asked you to cut a couple of sticks and be careful not to lose his knife."

"I see," said the farmer. "While we were walking over the city we did not see anybody that we knew, and not a soul gave us a scrap of anything to eat, till we were passing the cemetery; but there some people called to us and put into our hands some chapatis and kulchas; so my companion called the city a cemetery, and the cemetery a city."

"This also is to be understood, Father, if one thinks of the city as the place where everything is to be obtained, and of inhospitable people as worse than the dead. The city, though crowded with people, was as if dead, as far as you were concerned; while in the cemetery, which is crowded with the dead, you were saluted by kind friends and provided with bread."

"True, true!" said the astonished farmer. "Then, just now, when we were crossing the stream, he waded through it without taking off his shoes and robes."

"I admire his wisdom," replied the girl. "I have often thought how stupid people were to venture into that swiftly flowing stream and over those sharp stones with bare feet. The slightest stumble and they would fall, and be wetted from head to foot. This friend of yours is a most wise man. I should like to see him and speak to him."

"Very well," said the farmer; "I will go and find him, and bring him in."

"Tell him, Father, that our beams are strong enough, and then he will come in. I'll send on ahead a present to the man, to show him that we can afford to have him for our guest."

Accordingly she called a servant and sent him to the young man with a present of a basin of ghee, twelve chapatis, and a jar of milk, and the following message: "O friend, the moon is full; twelve months make a year, and the sea is overflowing with water."

Halfway the bearer of this present and message met his little son, who, seeing what was in the basket, begged his father to give him some of the food. His father foolishly complied. Presently he saw the young man, and gave him the rest of the present and the message.

"Give your mistress my salaam," he replied, "and tell her that the moon is new, and that I can only find eleven months in the year, and the sea is by no means full."

Not understanding the meaning of these words, the servant repeated them word for word, as he had heard them, to his mistress; and thus his theft was discovered, and he was severely punished. After a little while the young man appeared with the old farmer. Great attention was shown to him and he was treated in every way as if he were the son of a great man, although his humble host knew nothing of his origin. At length he told them everything—about the laughing of the fish, his father's threatened execution, and his own banishment—and asked their advice as to what he should do.

"The laughing of the fish," said the girl, "which seems to have been the cause of all this trouble, indicates that there is a man in the palace who is plotting against the King's life."

"Joy, joy!" exclaimed the vizier's son. "There is yet time for me to return and save my father from an ignominious and unjust death, and the King from danger."

The following day he hastened back to his own country, taking with him the farmer's daughter. Immediately on arrival he ran to the palace and informed his father of what he had heard. The poor vizier, now almost dead from the expectation of death, was at once carried to the King, to whom he repeated the news that his son had just brought.

"Never!" said the King.

"But it must be so, your Majesty," replied the vizier; "and in order to prove the truth of what I have heard, I pray you to call together all the maids in your palace, and order them to jump over a pit, which must be dug. We'll soon find out whether there is a man disguised as a maid."

The King had the pit dug, and commanded all the maids belonging to the palace to try to jump it. All of them tried, but only one succeeded. That one was found to be a man!

Thus was the Queen satisfied, and the faithful old vizier saved.

Afterwards, as soon as could be, the vizier's son married the old farmer's daughter; and a most happy marriage it was.

The Prince and the Flying Carpet

INDIA

Once upon a time there was a handsome prince who was very fond of hunting. Each day he would ride out in search of game. As it happened, though, there was one day when he had no luck. He stayed out until late afternoon and yet he still caught nothing. The prince continued to ride further and further, until he reached a dark jungle where he'd never been before. On a beautiful tree in this jungle he came upon a flock of parrots, perched upon the tree's branches. He quickly lifted his bow and took aim, but before he could shoot, there was a feathery rustle and a flurry of feathers and the parrots flew up and away into the sky. One parrot was left alone, sitting upon the branch.

"Do not shoot me!" said the bird. "For I am the raja of all parrots in the land. In return for leaving me, I will tell you about Princess Maya."

"Who is Princess Maya?" asked the prince, lowering his bow.

"Ahhh—the beautiful Princess Maya," said the parrot. "She is as radiant as the moon, as warm and gentle as the evening sun. In this great world she is beyond compare."

"But where is this Princess Maya?" asked the prince. "How can I find her?"

"You must go ever forward," said the parrot, "through many jungles and across wide plains. At the end of all this, you will find her."

That evening the prince rode home to the palace and thought of the beautiful princess. He made up his mind to find her, even if he had to search the whole world.

He bade goodbye to his parents, who were very sad; he was their only child, their golden treasure. But the prince had made up his mind and would not change it.

The very next morning, dressed in his finest clothes, carrying his bow and arrow and some food for the journey, he mounted his favorite horse and set off.

He rode to the dark jungle where he'd met the raja of parrots and then he rode forward, ever forward. He crossed wide plains and dark jungles. And still he rode on. Suddenly, he heard loud, angry voices. In a clearing nearby, he saw three demons—three small, sharp-eyed, wicked-looking demons, hissing at one another and circling round a small pile of things lying upon the ground. There was a bag, a stick, and an ancient carpet.

"Why are you fighting?" asked the prince.

One of the demons pointed to the things lying on the ground. "Our master died and left us these things," he said, "and I want all of them!"

"So do I!" shrieked the second demon.

"As do I!" howled the third.

"It is but a bag, a stick and an old carpet!" said the prince. "These things are not worth quarreling about."

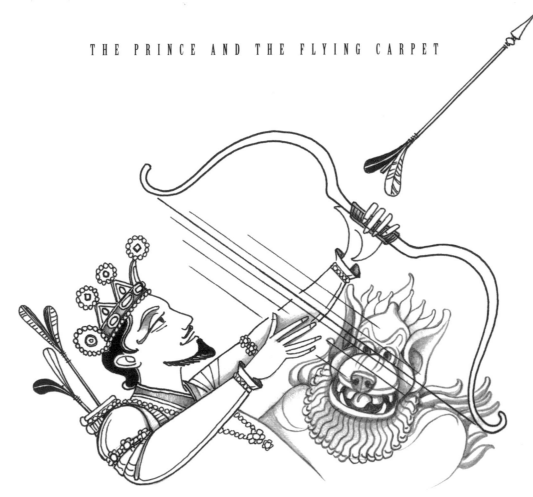

"Foolish man!" The first demon spat. "Not worth quarreling about! Why, the bag will give you anything you ask for. The stick will beat your enemies and—see the rope that is coiled around it?—that will tie them up so they can never escape. As for the carpet . . . it will take you anywhere you wish to go."

"Is that so?" said the prince, thinking quickly. "In that case, perhaps I could help you settle the quarrel," he suggested. "I will shoot three arrows into the air. The first one of you to find an arrow and bring it back here can have all of the treasures."

"Excellent!" the little demons agreed, their eyes sparkling. Each one was certain he was the fastest runner. Each was certain he would win the treasure.

So the prince let loose three arrows into the sky, and off the demons ran into the darkness of the jungle.

Then the prince jumped down from his horse, turned it round to face the way they had come, and said softly, "Lift your hooves, my fine friend, and gallop home!" And away the horse went.

The prince then picked up the stick and the bag, unrolled the carpet and sat down upon it, saying, "Carpet! Take me to the city where Princess Maya lives!"

The carpet rustled and shook, and then slowly it lifted itself upward. It rose slowly until they were higher than the trees and then it sailed forward through the air. It flew and flew and the prince looked below as dark jungles and wide plains passed beneath him. The carpet came to the edge of a great city, and then it gently floated downward.

When the carpet touched the gound, the prince stood up and looked about him. He rolled up the carpet and tucked it under his arm. Then, with the bag over his shoulder and the stick in his hand, he strode off into the city.

The first person he met was an old woman. "Tell me," he said to her, "Is this the city where Princess Maya lives?"

"Yes," she said.

"How can I find her?" he asked.

"You will see her at sunset," the old woman said, "for every night the princess comes out of the palace and sits on the roof for one hour, and she lights the city with her beauty."

That evening the prince waited outside the palace, and at sunset a slender maiden could be seen upon the roof of the palace. She wore a beautiful sari of shimmering silk and on her forehead was a delicate golden band, set with diamonds and pearls. A silvery radiance seemed to shine around her. In her presence night became day.

The prince could not take his eyes off of the beautiful Princess Maya. The raja parrot had been correct, for she was truly beyond compare.

That midnight, the prince looked to the bag upon his shoulder and said, "Bag! Give me a shawl of shimmering silk, to match the sari of Princess Maya!" And there—inside the bag—was a shawl of shimmering silk.

The prince unrolled his carpet and sat down, crossing his legs. "Carpet!" he said. "Take me to Princess Maya!"

Slowly the carpet rose until it was higher than the roofs. It floated gently until it reached the palace. Then it flew through an open window and landed softly upon the floor of Princess Maya's room.

The prince stepped off the carpet and saw the beautiful princess lying asleep in her bed. He placed the shimmering shawl on the pillow beside her head and then, quietly, he stepped back onto the carpet, and was off!

The next evening the prince again stood outside the palace and gazed at the beautiful princess. At midnight he said, "Bag! Give me a necklace of diamonds and pearls, the very match of the

Princess Maya's golden headband!" And there it was—a golden necklace set with diamonds and pearls.

Once again, the prince unrolled his carpet, sat down and said, "Carpet! Take me to Princess Maya!" Once in her room he placed the necklace beside the sleeping princess. Then—back on the carpet—and he was off!

The following evening the same things happened. The prince stood and gazed at the beautiful princess; and at midnight he said, "Bag! Give me a golden ring set with the finest diamonds in the world!" And there it was—a splendid and glittering ring.

Once again he unrolled his carpet and flew into the princess's room.

This time he did not place the gift beside the sleeping princess. Instead, he lifted her hand and slipped the ring upon her slender finger.

The princess stirred and opened her dark eyes. When she saw the handsome young prince who held her hand, she said, "So, you are the one who has given me the shawl and necklace, and now this ring. Tell me, is there something you wish for in return?"

"There is," said the prince. "Your hand in marriage is the gift I seek. Grant it me."

Princess Maya was surprised by the prince's soft words, but after they'd spoken together for much of the night, she agreed to marry the handsome, generous young man. In the morning she took him to her father, the raja of that land, and asked for his consent to their marriage.

But the raja was not pleased, for this man had stolen like a thief into his daughter's room. "You cannot marry him," he said.

The princess pleaded with her father until at last he agreed, provided the prince could prove that he was a man of strength and brave of heart.

"Outside the city there lives a fearsome ogre. He is as tall as two men, as broad as three and has the strength of six. My people live in fear of him. Daily he comes and kills and steals. If you can capture this ogre, then you can marry my daughter."

"I shall return, raja," said the prince. And bowing, he set off with the stick in his hand.

The prince had not gone far before the mighty ogre set upon him, roaring and bellowing in a great fury.

Brandishing the stick, the prince said, "Stick! Do your work!" And the stick went flying through the air and beat upon the ogre until he lay senseless upon the ground.

Then the prince said, "Rope! Do your work!" And the rope twirled itself from the stick and, quick as lightning, coiled itself round the ogre until he was bound, head to foot, so tight that not even a hair moved upon his back.

The prince returned to the raja's kingdom and the princess cheered. The raja then agreed to the marriage of the prince and his beautiful daughter, Princess Maya. There followed a great wedding of such feasting and rejoicing like none other throughout the land.

At last, it grew time for the prince to return to his own land with his new bride. A mighty procession led the couple's way out of the city. They rode splendid black horses and behind them trooped a hundred camels, their bells jingling, all laden with treasures the raja had heaped upon them.

And so the prince and princess returned to the royal stables. And what rejoicing there was, for his mother and father had presumed him dead. A huge celebration followed.

As the years passed, the prince and the beautiful Princess Maya lived happily and content together. The prince always kept the bag, the stick and carpet with him. And while the bag and the carpet were often useful, because they lived in a peaceful country the prince never again needed to use the stick.

The Hare's Liver

KOREA

Far below the rollicking waves of the sea there lived a great Dragon King in a beautiful palace. One day, the Dragon King, who had a mighty bellyache, rolled to and fro upon his huge bed of coral, and roared lustily of the horrible pain in his stomach. The Dragon King was surrounded by his Queen, Princesses and Princes, who took turns patting his great forehead and were generally very worried. All night long he groaned and tossed, and the waters of the sea churned to and fro with his roars. The following morning, he called his Cabinet Ministers into his chambers.

"I am quite ill, and it is even possible that I will soon have to throw away my spoon [die]. I have tried all the medicines my Kingdom has to offer, but alas, nothing can rid me of this pain. Who can cure my singular malady?" he bellowed.

From the crowd surrounding the Dragon King's bed, a lowly cuttlefish, the chief physician of the court, swam forward and reached out one of his tentacles to take the royal pulse. He then made a low bow to the King, cleared his throat, and said: "Your Majesty! You will be cured immediately upon eating the boiled liver of a hare. Long live the King!"

"Boiled liver of a hare!" exclaimed the Dragon King. "Who will fetch me this hare that I may have her liver plucked and boiled for my medicine?"

"Your Majesty!" said the swordfish, "I will pierce the hare with the mighty sword upon my nose and deliver this precious kebob to you myself."

"No!" roared the Dragon King. "The hare must be kept alive so her liver will be fresh."

"Your Majesty!" said the octopus. "I will capture the hare alive in my eight swimming arms and bring her to you fresh as the day she was born."

"Absolutely not!" thundered the Dragon King, "The grip of your eight tentacles will surely crush her tender liver. Who will fetch me my hare?"

All was silent in the watery kindgom. At last, the turtle stepped slowly forward and prostrated himself before the Dragon King. He struck his head upon the floor three times, and then said, "Sire, allow me to fetch you the hare using only the shell upon my back. I will thusly carry the hare and bring her safely back to Your Majesty."

"Excellent!" roared the Dragon King. "I recall that your grandfather, in his youth, once ran a race with a hare. And victory was his. Again, the spoils shall be ours! You can travel both on land and sea. Go and fetch me the hare. I shall neither rest nor eat until I have eaten the hare's boiled liver! Artists! Draw a life-like portrait of the hare so the turtle makes no mistake and brings back the correct animal."

The court artists immediately set to drawing the portrait of the hare. One drew eyes that saw all the beauties of nature, one drew ears that heard the songs of the birds and the trees, one drew a mouth that ate orchids and fragrant herbs, one drew a snow-white fleece shielding the wintry blast, and one drew legs bouncing in the clouds that hung over high hills and deep valleys. When the portrait was finally finished, it looked exactly like a

living hare with two round pink eyes, forelegs short and hind legs long, and two ears perked up into the air.

The turtle took the portrait, hung it from a chain around his neck and took leave of the watery kingdom. The Dragon Princesses waved sad handkerchiefs at his back as he swam to the surface of the blue sea. He let himself drift aimlessly upon the waves and after a long trip, he was happy when he spotted land. The turtle lumbered ashore on his short little legs and continued on toward a beautiful mountain in the distance, and a melodious stream.

It was spring on the land, and all was bright and gay. The creatures bounced along the grass, the azaleas breathed their sweet perfume, the butterflies flirted from flower to flower, the apple blossoms dappled over deep sapphire pools, birds sang sweetly to one another, swallows twittered their return from the warm south, while cuckoos and thousands of other birds warbled in their sweetest voices. All the land was shining and bright with lovely pink flowers and flowing silvery streams.

Stopping to smell the flowers and drink from the fresh streams, the turtle continued up the hill looking for traces of the hare.

After some time, a rumbling of sound approached him. Suddenly, a crowd of animals appeared running down the hill— squrrels, deer, wolves, bears, wild boars, tigers, panthers, weasels, monkeys, elephants, and foxes ... but not a hare to be found.

The turtle stretched his great neck and looked all about him, and at last, his eyes rested upon a pretty creature who largely resembled the portrait he had hung about his neck. He looked again at this creature and then at the portrait, and in this way he assured himself that this was the animal he sought. He was very happy indeed, and for some time he simply watched the movements of the hare. She nibbled at the fresh grass, leapt onto hanging rocks and generally danced round and round.

Finally, the turtle cleared his wrinkly throat and addressed her in the following, flattering speech: "My dear Miss Hare. I wish you a lovely morning. I have heard so much of your very own fragrant name but until this moment I've never had the distinct pleasure of seeing you, even once, in my life. How very happy indeed I am to have met you here today in this most beautiful spring!"

Whereupon the hare replied: "I have traveled all over the earth but never have I come across such an ugly creature as you! Your toeless feet, your wrinkly neck sliding back and forth, your back, rugged and round—how strange. At first, I thought you were a wooden bowl. Who in the world are you?"

The turtle, naturally, was not at all pleased with these nasty remarks, but controlled his temper admirably and answered: "My name is Turtle, though most know me as Byuljoobo. My back is round so that I will never sink while floating in the waves; my neck is long so I may see far and wide; my body is round so that I can behave as an all-round perfect gentleman. I am the hero of the water and captain of the sea creatures. I assure you I come from excellent stock.

"You, however, dear Miss Hare, are very proud of your wide travels. But you have never seen the bottom of the sea, now have you? Have you ever seen the sea's beautiful plants, its coral, its fish, its perfect aquatic beauty? Have you ever seen the water palace of the Dragon King? Hop onto my back and I will show you all of these wonders and more. The Dragon King will treat you like a princess."

The hare was thrilled by the turtle's description and immediately hopped upon his back. They traveled back to the sea and the turtle took a great long, deep dive, and brought her safely to the water palace underneath the South Sea.

The turtle brought the hare to a magnificent ante-chamber adjoining the audience hall. Here she was instructed to wait and be received by the Dragon King. Suddenly, an army of soldiers rushed in, bound her hands and feet and, crying "Long live the King! Long live the King!," they carried her before the dragon throne.

The hare trembled from her whiskers to her tail; her astonishment was beyond description. Before her was a monstrous green beast with a coral and pearl crown glittering upon his head. A long silvery robe of fish fins flowed over his horny body, two fiery eyes flashed upon his brow, and a pearl scepter sparkled in his awesome hands. He sat upon a throne, surrounded by hundreds of officers. His huge mouth, with massive pointy teeth, was open, and a long forked crimson tongue lolled down, ready to swallow the hare in

a single mouthful. This was the Dragon King and in his thundering way, he declared the following message to the hare:

"Listen, hare! I am the Great King of the Sea. You, you are merely a small creature of the hill. I am suffering from an unusual malady whose cure alone is your very own boiled liver. I have sent this turtle to bring you here in order that your liver will cure my disease. In order to do this you must die. I expect you not to regret your death. For upon your death, my servants will shroud you with fine silks and jewels and lay you in a glorious casket of divine beauty. Your name and your sacrifice will become the stuff of legends for it is you and you alone that have cured the ailment of a king. A shrine will be erected in your honor and you will always be remembered. You are fortunate to die such a glorious death. It is far better than to become the prey of a tiger or hunter on the hill. You may now thank me for this honor and prepare to die with a happy expression."

Rolling his eyes to the left and to the right, the Dragon King then commanded his servants to split the belly of the hare and remove her liver. The ferocious soldiers rushed forward, brandishing their swords.

This speech was a particularly shocking bolt from the blue, and the poor little hare would have fainted dead away had not she kept her great presence of mind. Summoning all of her courage and wit, she spoke to the Dragon King in a very serious voice:

"Your Majesty! Permit me to make a brief farewell address! A humble creature such as myself would gladly embrace death to restore the health of such a noble monarch! I regret to say, alas, that it is my sorrow to report that I am the daughter of a hare and a star in the Milky Way, conceived of a celestial spirit. From the very moment of my birth, I have sipped morning dew and eaten fragrant grass together with medicinal herbs. By and by, my liver has become a wonderful remedy that could cure all, in addition to giving perpetual youth to he who partakes of it. All the people on the land have begged me to give them my liver to eat. It is as a result of this constant begging that I was forced to pluck my own liver, together with my own heart, with my own hands, washed them many times in a clean mountain stream, and hide them in a secret place upon the hill. Unexpectedly I met the turtle upon my return from this journey and traveled on his back to your palace. Had I only known of your singular malady, I surely would have brought my liver with me . . . ."

The Dragon King was struck dumb. He wondered whether her words were true. He roared:

"How can you pull out your very own liver and push it back so easily?"

Now almost sure of her escape, the hare answered: "The Heaven was opened in the hour of the rat, the Earth was formed in the hour of the cow, the first man was born in the hour of the tiger, and all creatures came out in the hour of the hare. Therefore, I am above ten thousand birds and animals. Even the benevolent giraffe and the noble phoenix bow and sing of my work. Can I not play at such easy magic as removing and replacing the liver in my own body?"

The Dragon King was silent as he pondered the hare's words. "I cannot kill a fair creature if she does not have what it is I seek. Then there would be no one to lead me to her liver hiding upon the hill. I had better send her home to bring it back. She is so earnest of voice; indeed, she cannot be telling a lie," he said to himself. So he gave the hare two hundred sparkling pearls and spoke in a mild and gentle voice:

"Take these beautiful gifts as a souvenir of your first visit to my water palace. Go in peace and return with your liver."

The hare placed the pearls in a pouch and, with a bow, she mounted the back of the turtle and began her homeward voyage.

After rolling through the waves and once again reaching the hills, the turtle tossed his fair rider upon the shore.

"Now go and get your liver. I will await you. We will then return to the watery palace immediately."

The hare laughed heartily until her sides almost split and she nearly did toss out her liver.

"What a fool you are!" she cried. "Now I truly understand the phrase 'foolish as a turtle.' I fooled your Dragon King and the whole court! Do you still believe I can push my liver in and out like a toy? Whatever it is that is ailing your Dragon King has nothing to do with me. Your fine kidnapping trick makes me want to kill you, but being the most excellent hare that I am, I will

pardon your crime and spare you your life. Now go back and tell your Dragon King to forget my liver, and kiss death with a glad heart, for no medicine can guarantee immortal life or forever keep away death, for death embraces prince and peasant as equals once the hour is upon us.

Again the hare laughed and, clutching the pearls in her sack, she trotted into the forest to be seen nevermore.

The Storyteller at Fault

IRELAND

At the time when the Tuatha De Danann[1] held the sovereignty of Ireland, there reigned in Leinster a king, who was remarkably fond of hearing stories. Like the other princes and chieftains of the island, he had a favorite storyteller, who held a large estate from his Majesty, on condition of telling him a new story every night of his life, before he went to sleep. Many indeed were the stories he knew, so that he had already reached a good old age without failing even for a single night in his task; and such was the skill he displayed that whatever cares of state or other annoyances might prey upon the monarch's mind, his storyteller was sure to send him to sleep.

One morning the storyteller arose early, and as his custom was, strolled out into his garden, turning over in his mind incidents that he might weave into a story for the king at night. But this morning he found himself quite at fault; after pacing his whole demesne, he

---

[1]   One of the five races that originally invaded and inhabited prehistoric Ireland.

returned to his house without being able to think of anything new or strange. He found no difficulty in "there was once a king who had three sons," or "one day the king of all Ireland," but further than that he could not get. At length he went in to breakfast, and found his wife much perplexed at his delay.

"Why don't you come to breakfast, my dear?" said she.

"I have no mind to eat anything," replied the storyteller, "for as long as I have been in the service of the king of Leinster, I never sat down to breakfast without having a new story ready for the evening, but this morning my mind is quite shut up, and I don't know what to do. I might as well lie down and die at once. I'll be disgraced forever this evening, when the king calls for his storyteller."

Just at this moment the lady looked out of the window.

"Do you see that black thing at the end of the field?" said she.

"I do," replied her husband.

They drew nigh, and saw a miserable-looking old man lying on the ground with a wooden leg placed beside him.

"Who are you, my good man?" asked the storyteller.

"Oh, then, 'tis little matter who I am. I'm a poor, old, lame, decrepit, miserable creature, sitting down here to rest a while."

"And what are you doing with that box and dice I see in your hand?"

"I am waiting here to see if anyone will play a game with me," replied the beggarman.

"Play with you! Why what has a poor old man like you to play for?"

"I have one hundred pieces of gold in this leather purse," replied the old man.

"You may as well play with him," said the storyteller's wife, "and perhaps you'll have something to tell the king in the evening."

A smooth stone was placed between them, and upon it they cast their throws.

In a little while, the storyteller lost every penny of his money.

"Much good may it do you, friend," said he. "What better luck could I look for, fool that I am!"

"Will you play again?" asked the old man.

"Don't be talking, man; you have all my money."

"Haven't you chariot and horses and hounds?"

"Well, what of them?"

"I'll stake all the money I have against them."

"Nonsense, man! Do you think for all the money in Ireland I'd run the risk of seeing my lady tramp home on foot?"

"Maybe you'd win," said the beggar.

"Maybe I wouldn't," said the storyteller.

"Play with him, husband," said his wife. "I don't mind walking, if you lose, love."

"I never refused you before," said the storyteller, "and I won't do so now."

Down he sat again, and in one throw lost horses, hounds, and chariot.

"Will you play again?" asked the beggar.

"Are you making game of me, man; what else have I to stake?"

"I'll stake all my winnings against your wife," said the old man.

The storyteller turned away in silence, but his wife stopped him.

"Accept his offer," said she. "This is the third time, and who knows what luck you may have? You'll surely win now."

They played again, and the storyteller lost. No sooner had he done so than, to his sorrow and surprise, his wife went and sat down near the ugly old beggar.

"Is that the way you're leaving me?" asked the storyteller.

"Sure I was won," said she. "You would not cheat the poor man, would you?"

"Have you any more to stake?" asked the old man.

"You know very well I have not," replied the storyteller.

"I'll stake the whole now, wife and all, against your own self," said the old man.

Again they played, and again the storyteller lost.

"Well! Here I am, and what do you want with me?"

"I'll soon let you know," said the old man, and he took from his pocket a long cord and a wand.

"Now," said he to the storyteller, "what kind of animal would you rather be: a deer, a fox, or a hare? You have your choice now, but you may not have it later."

To make a long story short, the storyteller made his choice of a hare; the old man threw the cord round him, struck him with the wand, and lo! a long-eared, frisking hare was skipping and jumping on the green.

But it wasn't for long; who but his wife called the hounds, and set them on him. The hare fled, the dogs followed. Round the field ran a high wall, so that, run as he might, he couldn't get out, and mightily diverted were beggar and lady to see him twist and double.

In vain did he take refuge with his wife, for she kicked him back again to the hounds, until at length the beggar stopped the hounds, and with a stroke of the wand, panting and breathless, the storyteller stood before them again.

"And how did you like the sport?" said the beggar.

"It might be sport to others," replied the storyteller, looking at his wife. "For my part I could well put up with the loss of it.

"Would it be asking too much," he went on to the beggar, "to know who you are at all, or where you come from, or why you take a pleasure in plaguing a poor old man like me?"

"Oh!" replied the stranger. "I'm an odd kind of good-for-little fellow, one day poor, another day rich, but if you wish to know more about me or my habits come with me and perhaps I may show you more than you would make out if you went alone."

"I'm not my own master to go or stay," said the storyteller, with a sigh.

The stranger put one hand into his wallet and drew out of it before their eyes a good-looking middle-aged man, to whom he spoke as follows:

"By all you heard and saw since I put you into my wallet, take charge of this lady and of the carriage and horses, and have them ready for me whenever I want them."

Scarcely had he said these words when all vanished, and the storyteller found himself at the Foxes' Ford, near the castle of Red Hugh O'Donnell. He could see all but none could see him.

O'Donnell was in his hall, and heaviness of flesh and weariness of spirit were upon him.

"Go out," said he to his doorkeeper, "and see who or what may be coming."

The doorkeeper went, and what he saw was a lank, gray beggarman; half his sword bared behind his haunch, his two shoes full of cold water sousing about him, the tips of his two ears out through his old hat, his two shoulders out through his scant, tattered cloak, and in his hand a green wand of holly.

"Save you, O'Donnell," said the lank, gray beggarman.

"And you likewise," said O'Donnell. "Whence come you, and what is your craft?"

"I come from the outmost stream of earth,
From the glens where the white swans glide.
A night in Islay, a night in Man,
A night on the cold hillside."

"It's the great traveler you are," said O'Donnell. "Maybe you've learned something on the road."

"I am a juggler," said the lank, gray beggarman, "and for five pieces of silver you shall see a trick of mine."

"You shall have them," said O'Donnell; and the lank, gray beggarman took three small straws and placed them in his hand.

"The middle one," said he, "I'll blow away; the other two I'll leave."

"You cannot do it," said one and all.

But the lank, gray beggarman put a finger on either outside straw and, whiff, away he blew the middle one.

"'Tis a good trick," said O'Donnell; and he paid him his five pieces of silver.

"For half the money," said one of the chief's lads, "I'll do the same trick."

"Take him at his word, O'Donnell."

The lad put the three straws on his hand, and a finger on either outside straw and he blew; and what happened but that the fist was blown away with the straw.

"You are sore, and you will be sorer," said O'Donnell.

"Six more pieces, O'Donnell, and I'll do another trick for you," said the lank, gray beggarman.

"Six you shall have."

"See my two ears! One I'll move but not the other."

"'Tis easy to see them, they're big enough, but you can never move one ear and not the two together."

The lank, gray beggarman put his hand to his ear, and he gave it a pull.

O'Donnell laughed and paid him the six pieces.

"Call that a trick?" said the fistless lad. "Anyone can do that," and, so saying, he put up his hand, pulled his ear, and what happened was that he pulled away ear and hand.

"Sore you are, and sorer you will be," said O'Donnell.

"Well, O'Donnell," said the lank, gray beggarman, "strange are the tricks I've shown you, but I'll show you a stranger one yet for the same money."

"You have my word for it," said O'Donnell.

With that, the lank, gray beggarman took a bag from under his armpit, and from the bag a ball of silk, and he unwound the ball and he flung it slantwise up into the clear blue heavens, and it became a ladder; then he took a hare and placed it upon the thread, and up it ran; again he took out a red-eared hound, and it swiftly ran up after the hare.

"Now," said the lank, gray beggarman, "has anyone a mind to run after the dog and on the course?"

"I will," said a lad of O'Donnell's.

"Up with you, then," said the juggler, "but I warn you if you let my hare be killed I'll cut off your head when you come down."

The lad ran up the thread, and all three soon disappeared. After looking up for a long time, the lank, gray beggarman said, "I'm afraid the hound is eating the hare, and that our friend has fallen asleep."

Saying this, he began to wind the thread, and down came the lad fast asleep, and down came the red-eared hound and in his mouth the last morsel of the hare.

He struck the lad a stroke with the edge of his sword, and so cast his head off. As for the hound, if he used it no worse, he used it no better.

"It's little I'm pleased, and much I'm angered," said O'Donnell, "that a hound and a lad should be killed at my court."

"Five pieces of silver twice over for each of them," said the juggler, "and their heads shall be on them as before."

"That I will give you," said O'Donnell.

Five pieces and again five were paid him, and lo! the lad had his head and the hound his. And though they lived to the uttermost end of time, the hound would never touch a hare again, and the lad took good care to keep his eyes open.

Scarcely had the lank, gray beggarman done this when he vanished from their sight, and no one present could say if he had flown through the air or if the earth had swallowed him up.

> *"He moved as wave tumbling o'er wave*
> *As whirlwind following whirlwind,*
> *As a furious wintry blast,*
> *So swiftly, sprucely, cheerily,*
> *Right proudly,*
> *And no stop made*
> *Until he came*
> *To the court of Leinster's King,*
> *He gave a cheery light leap*
> *O'er top of turret,*
> *Of court and city*
> *Of Leinster's King."*

Heavy was the flesh and weary the spirit of Leinster's king. 'Twas the hour he was used to hear a story, but send he might right and left, not a jot of tidings about the storyteller could he get.

"Go to the door," said he to his doorkeeper, "and see if a soul is in sight who may tell me something about my storyteller."

The doorkeeper went, and what he saw was a lank, gray beggarman, half his sword bared behind his haunch, his two old shoes full of cold water sousing about him, the tips of his two ears out through his old hat, his two shoulders out through his scant, tattered cloak, and in his hand a three-stringed harp.

"What can you do?" said the doorkeeper.

"I can play," said the lank, gray beggarman.

"Never fear," added he to the storyteller, "you shall see all, but not a man shall see you."

When the king heard a harper was outside he bade him in.

"It is I that have the best harpers in the five-fifths of Ireland," said he, and he signaled them to play. They did so, and if they played, the lank, gray beggarman listened.

"Have you ever heard the like?" said the king.

"Did you ever, O King, hear a cat purring over a bowl of broth, or the buzzing of beetles in the twilight, or a shrill-tongued old woman scolding your head off?"

"That I have often," said the king.

"More melodious to me," said the lank, gray beggarman, "were the worst of these sounds than the sweetest harping of your harpers."

When the harpers heard this, they drew their swords and rushed at him, but instead of striking him, their blows fell on each other, and soon each man was cracking his neighbor's skull and getting his own cracked in turn.

When the king saw this, he thought it hard the harpers weren't content with murdering their music, but must murder each other.

"Hang the fellow who began it all," said he, "and if I can't have a story, let me have peace."

Up came the guards, seized the lank, gray beggarman, marched him to the gallows and hanged him high and dry. Back they

marched to the hall, and who should they see but the lank, gray beggarman seated on a bench with his mouth to a flagon of ale.

"Never welcome you in," cried the captain of the guard. "Didn't we hang you this minute, and what brings you here?"

"Is it me myself, you mean?"

"Who else?" said the captain.

"May your hand turn into a pig's foot when you think of tying the rope; why should you speak of hanging me?"

Back they scurried to the gallows, and there hung the king's favorite brother.

Back they hurried to the king who had fallen fast asleep.

"Please, your Majesty," said the captain, "we hanged that strolling vagabond, but here he is back again as well as ever."

"Hang him again," said the king, and off he went to sleep once more.

They did as they were told, but what happened was that they found the king's chief harper hanging where the lank, gray beggarman should have been.

The captain of the guard was sorely puzzled.

"Are you wishful to hang me a third time?" said the lank, gray beggarman.

"Go where you will," said the captain, "and as fast as you please if you'll only go far enough. It's trouble enough you've given us already."

"Now you're reasonable," said the beggarman, "and since you've given up trying to hang a stranger because he finds fault with your music, I don't mind telling you that if you go back to the gallows you'll find your friends sitting on the sward none the worse for what has happened."

As he said these words he vanished; and the storyteller found himself on the spot where they first met, and where his wife still was with the carriage and horses.

"Now," said the lank, gray beggarman, "I'll torment you no longer. There's your carriage and your horses, and your money and your wife: do what you please with them."

"For my carriage and my horses and my hounds," said the storyteller, "I thank you; but my wife and my money you may keep."

"No," said the other. "I want neither, and as for your wife, don't think ill of her for what she did, she couldn't help it."

"Not help it! Not help kicking me into the mouth of my own hounds! Not help casting me off for the sake of a beggarly old—"

"I'm not as beggarly or as old as you think. I am Angus of the Bruff; many a good turn you've done me with the king of Leinster. This morning my magic told me the difficulty you were in, and I made up my mind to get you out of it. As for your wife there, the

power that changed your body changed her mind. Forget and forgive as man and wife should do, and now you have a story for the king of Leinster when he calls for one." With that he disappeared.

It's true enough he now had a story fit for a king. From first to last he told all that had befallen him, so long and loud laughed the king that he couldn't go to sleep at all. And he told the storyteller never to trouble for fresh stories, but every night as long as he lived he listened again and he laughed afresh at the tale of the lank, gray beggarman.

The Man Who Loved Flowers

CHINA

It must have been twelve hundred years ago that Tsui Hsuan-wei lived in the Middle Kingdom. He was one who sought to make himself perfect, and the way he chose to do this was a good way. He built for himself a small house, and around it there was laid out a beautiful garden. And in this modest house, within his garden wall, Hsuan-wei lived alone in peace and contentment, enjoying the benefit of good thoughts.

The garden was gay with flowers; and this good man loved nothing more than to walk among them, tending them and admiring their fresh beauty.

One night a round, honey-colored moon hung in the sky, and the air was soft and still. As Hsuan-wei walked slowly amongst the fragrance of his flowers, he saw a maiden coming in a shy manner toward him in the moonlight.

Hsuan-wei was surprised, almost alarmed, at this sight. It was many years since any person had come unbidden into his garden.

While he watched, the maiden came nearer to him and finally stood meekly in front of him, her head downcast, her dark eyelashes fluttering with excitement.

Her behavior was very correct, and Hsuan-wei was a little reassured; so, when she had bowed respectfully before him, he asked her kindly who she might be, and what she was doing there at this hour.

The maiden lifted to him a face of bright loveliness. "I live close by," she said. "My friends and I come this way tonight to visit our Auntie Feng. We beg that we may rest for a while in your garden."

Hsuan-wei gladly agreed to this suggestion, and at once the maiden's companions appeared, so they must have been very close by all this time. They were a laughing, graceful group of young ladies, each dressed in a different color.

As they bowed, they gaily introduced themselves.

"I am Willow," said a girl in green.

"I am Plum," said one all in white.

"And I Chrysanthemum," laughed a plump little one in purple.

This went on for quite a time; for there must have been twenty or thirty maidens. The last to announce herself was one dressed in red. Her name was Pomegranate.

This young woman seemed to have more confidence than the rest. "We had hoped to see our Auntie Feng tonight," she told Hsuan-wei, "but she did not come. We therefore thought that we would go to visit her; and then it seemed that it would be delightful to stop and pay you some few compliments, because you have always been kind to us."

While they were yet talking, Auntie Feng appeared. She was a thin-featured woman with a chilling glance. Indeed, Hsuan-wei felt quite cold at the sight of her.

When this lady had been presented to him by the chattering

maidens, Hsuan-wei made instant preparations for a small feast; and in quite a short time they were all seated in his house and enjoying fine foods and rare wines. The moon shone more and more brightly, and the room was so filled with fragrance that it seemed almost as if all the flowers in the garden had crowded inside.

Pomegranate filled a large cup of wine and presented it to Auntie Feng, the chief guest. Then, glowing in her red robe, she sang a song. It was about the sad shortness of youth, and of how it was useless to blame the wind for this, when it was something that just had to happen.

The song was very well received by the maidens and by their host, who exclaimed, "Good! Good!" in a warm voice. But Auntie Feng did not show any pleasure.

Then Plum, very white in the moon's radiance, sang a song. And this, too, was about how one was young and fresh for such a little time, and how useless it was to reproach the harsh wind for this.

While this song was being sung, Auntie Feng, who had not touched the cup of wine that Plum had first presented to her, began to look very cold indeed. And when Plum had finished, and the maidens had all expressed their pleasure, Auntie Feng spoke.

"I cannot think," she said frigidly, "why you should choose to sing such dismal songs in a gathering so agreeable as this. Please do not imagine that I have not noticed the criticism of myself in the words you have sung. Now, as a punishment, you, Pomegranate, and you, Plum, must each drink a large cup of wine; and then sing a song about cheerful matters." And, saying this, Auntie Feng filled two cups with wine and handed them to the abashed girls.

It was very unfortunate that one cup should be spilled, and even more unfortunate that it should be spilled over the red dress of Pomegranate. For Pomegranate was not only very careful of her gowns, but she was also (alas!) a little high-spirited.

Instead of accepting the rebuke of an elder person with cheerfulness, she quite lost her temper.

"The others may be afraid of you," she said impertinently to Auntie Feng, "but I am not." And with that she stalked out of the room with as much firmness as a young person so soft and frail can manage.

Auntie Feng was very angry. She got up from the table. "Who is this impertinent young girl," she demanded, "who dares to speak to me in such a fashion?"

The other girls tried at once to pacify her. "She is but young and ignorant. She will repent and ask your pardon in the morning."

Hsuan-wei, too, did all that he could to restore good humor to Auntie Feng; but no one could calm her anger. Still cold with rage, she went away. And when Auntie Feng departed, so did all the pretty maidens. At one moment the room was a jostle of excited girls; the next moment it was empty. The moon had slipped down, and the warm scent of flowers was gone.

The host, hoping at least to part with his guests in a seemly manner, ran out into the garden to catch them and give them parting greetings; but in the darkness he tripped over a stone, and by the time he had gotten to his feet again the voices of his visitors had faded away.

However, the next evening Hsuan-wei was in his garden as soon as it was dusk. He was very pleased to find that the maidens were already there. They stood in a glimmering group scolding Pomegranate, and trying to persuade her to apologize to Auntie Feng.

When Pomegranate saw Hsuan-wei approach, she broke away from the group of girls and ran lightly to him. Then, placing herself a little behind him, she said to the others from around his elbow, "Why should we trouble ourselves to apologize to Auntie Feng, when our good friend here can protect us?"

This suggestion seemed to please her friends. At once they gave up chiding Pomegranate, and, laughing and chattering, ran up to their host and looked up at him expectantly.

A little alarmed at this situation, Hsuan-wei asked hopelessly: "But in what way can I protect you?"

"Oh! It is a very simple matter," Pomegranate assured him. "You have only to make a banner; and on the banner must be painted the sun and the moon and the four constellations. On the first morning when there is a wind from the east, you must set up this banner in the eastern part of your garden. In this way you will protect us."

Hsuan-wei willingly promised to do this; and, no sooner had he promised than the maidens vanished away. When he stared

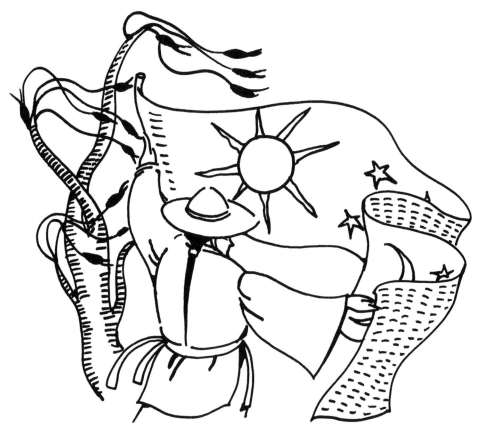

about him, all he could see were tree blossoms and garden flowers nodding to him as if they were friends.

That very day Hsuan-wei made the banner, and on the first morning when a light breeze from the east stirred the flowers, he set it up firmly in the eastern part of the garden.

The light breeze freshened, and then began to blow until the tall trees outside the garden seemed to clap their hands and rock upon their feet. It blew until roofs rattled and branches snapped. In the countryside whole forests were uprooted, and river waters were blown upstream. But inside Hsuan-wei's garden, where the magic banner hung listless, not a breath of wind disturbed the trees and flowers.

Hsuan-wei could see now clearly that Auntie Feng was none other than the east wind, and that the little ladies were in truth flowers themselves. But this did not lead him to treat their advice lightly when, after the storm was passed, the lively maidens came running in the evening to thank him.

They were all there in their bright colors. Each brought him a handful of flower petals.

"To eat," each one said prettily as she pressed the petals into his hands.

"To eat," said Pomegranate, coming last of all in her red gown. "To eat." Her voice was as clear as trickling water. "It will keep off old age."

And when Hsuan-wei did faithfully eat all those petals, it must be said that he at once began to look like a young man. And with the time he thus gained, and because of his virtuous life, he did at last become an Immortal.

Momotaro, or The Story of the Son of a Peach

JAPAN

L ong, long ago there lived an old man and an old woman; they were peasants, and had to work hard to earn their daily rice. The old man used to go and cut grass for the farmers around, and while he was gone the old woman, his wife, did the work of the house and worked in their own little rice field.

One day the old man went to the hills as usual to cut grass and the old woman took some clothes to the river to wash.

It was nearly summer, and the country was very beautiful to see in its fresh greenness as the two old people went on their way to work. The grass on the banks of the river looked like emerald velvet, and the pussy willows along the edge of the water were shaking out their soft tassels.

The breezes blew and ruffled the smooth surface of the water into wavelets, and passing on touched the cheeks of the old couple who, for some reason they could not explain, felt very happy that morning.

The old woman at last found a nice spot by the riverbank and put her basket down. Then she set to work to wash the clothes; she took them one by one out of the basket and washed them in the river and rubbed them on the stones. The water was as clear as crystal, and she could see the tiny fish swimming to and fro, and the pebbles at the bottom.

As she was busy washing her clothes a great peach came bumping down the stream. The old woman looked up from her work and saw this large peach. She was sixty years of age, yet in all her life she had never seen such a big peach as this.

"How delicious that peach must be!" she said to herself. "I must certainly get it and take it home to my husband."

She stretched out her arm to try to get it, but it was quite out of her reach. She looked about for a stick, but there was not one to be seen, and if she went to look for one she would lose the peach.

Stopping a moment to think what she would do, she remembered an old charm-verse. Now she began to clap her hands to keep time to the rolling of the peach down the stream, and while she clapped she sang this song:

> *"Distant water is bitter,*
> *The near water is sweet;*
> *Pass by the distant water*
> *And come into the sweet."*

Strange to say, as soon as she began to repeat this little song the peach began to come nearer and nearer the bank where the old woman was standing, till at last it stopped just in front of her so that she was able to take it up in her hands. The old woman was delighted. She could not go on with her work, so happy and excited was she, so she put all the clothes back in her bamboo basket, and with the basket on her back and the peach in her hand she hurried homeward.

It seemed a very long time to her to wait till her husband returned. The old man at last came back as the sun was setting, with a big bundle of grass on his back—so big that he was almost hidden and she could hardly see him. He seemed very tired and used the scythe for a walking stick, leaning on it as he walked along.

As soon as the old woman saw him she called out:

"O *Jii San* [old man]! I have been waiting for you to come home for such a long time today!"

"What is the matter? Why are you so impatient?" asked the old man, wondering at her unusual eagerness. "Has anything happened while I have been away?"

"Oh, no!" answered the old woman. "Nothing has happened, only I have found a nice present for you!"

"That is good," said the old man. He then washed his feet in a basin of water and stepped up to the veranda.

The old woman now ran into the little room and brought out from the cupboard the big peach. It felt even heavier than before. She held it up to him, saying:

"Just look at this! Did you ever see such a large peach in all your life?"

When the old man looked at the peach he was greatly astonished and said:

"This is indeed the largest peach I have ever seen! Wherever did you buy it?"

"I did not buy it," answered the old woman. "I found it in the river where I was washing." And she told him the whole story.

"I am very glad that you have found it. Let us eat it now, for I am hungry," said the O *Jii San*.

He brought out the kitchen knife and, placing the peach on a board, was about to cut it when, wonderful to tell, the peach split in two of itself and a clear voice said:

"Wait a bit, old man!" and out stepped a beautiful little child.

The old man and his wife were both so astonished at what they saw that they fell to the ground. The child spoke again:

"Don't be afraid. I am no demon or fairy. I will tell you the truth. Heaven has had compassion on you. Every day and every night you have lamented that you had no child. Your cry has been heard and I am sent to be the son of your old age!"

On hearing this the old man and his wife were very happy. They had cried night and day for sorrow at having no child to help them in their lonely old age, and now that their prayer was answered they were so lost with joy that they did not know where to put their hands or their feet. First the old man took the child up in his arms, and then the old woman did the same; and they named him *Momotaro*, or *Son of a Peach*, because he had come out of a peach.

The years passed quickly by and the child grew to be fifteen years of age. He was taller and far stronger than any other boys of his own age, he had a handsome face and a heart full of courage, and he was very wise for his years. The old couple's pleasure was very great when they looked at him, for he was just what they thought a hero ought to be like.

One day Momotaro came to his foster-father and said solemnly:

"Father, by a strange chance we have become father and son. Your goodness to me has been higher than the mountain grasses

which it was your daily work to cut, and deeper than the river where my mother washes the clothes. I do not know how to thank you enough."

"Why," answered the old man, "it is a matter of course that a father should bring up his son. When you are older it will be your turn to take care of us, so after all there will be no profit or loss between us—all will be equal. Indeed, I am rather surprised that you should thank me in this way!" and the old man looked bothered.

"I hope you will be patient with me," said Momotaro, "but before I begin to pay back your goodness to me I have a request to make which I hope you will grant me above everything else."

"I will let you do whatever you wish, for you are quite different from all other boys!"

"Then let me go away at once!"

"What do you say? Do you wish to leave your old father and mother and go away from your old home?"

"I will surely come back again, if you let me go now!"

"Where are you going?"

"You must think it strange that I want to go away," said Momotaro, "because I have not yet told you my reason. Far away from here to the northeast of Japan there is an island in the sea. This island is the stronghold of a band of devils. I have often heard how they invade this land, kill and rob the people, and carry off all they can find. They are not only very wicked but they are disloyal to our emperor and disobey his laws. They are also cannibals, for they kill and eat some of the poor people who are so unfortunate as to fall into their hands. These devils are very hateful beings. I must go and conquer them and bring back all the plunder of which they have robbed this land. It is for this reason that I want to go away for a short time!"

The old man was much surprised at hearing all this from a mere boy of fifteen. He thought it best to let the boy go. He was strong and fearless, and besides all this, the old man knew he was no common child, for he had been sent to them as a gift from Heaven, and he felt quite sure that the devils would be powerless to harm him.

"All you say is very interesting, Momotaro," said the old man. "I will not hinder you in your determination. You may go if you wish. Go to the island as soon as ever you like and destroy the demons and bring peace to the land."

"Thank you, for all your kindness," said Momotaro, who began to get ready to go that very day. He was full of courage and did not know what fear was.

The old man and woman at once set to work to pound rice in the kitchen mortar to make cakes for Momotaro to take with him on his journey.

At last the cakes were made and Momotaro was ready to start on his long journey.

Parting is always sad. So it was now. The eyes of the two old people were filled with tears and their voices trembled as they said:

"Go with all care and speed. We expect you back victorious!"

Momotaro was very sorry to leave his old parents (though he knew he was coming back as soon as he could) for he thought of how lonely they would be while he was away. But he said "Goodbye!" quite bravely.

"I am going now. Take good care of yourselves while I am away. Goodbye!" And he stepped quickly out of the house. In silence the eyes of Momotaro and his parents met in farewell.

Momotaro now hurried on his way till it was midday. He

began to feel hungry, so he opened his bag and took out one of the rice cakes and sat down under a tree by the side of the road to eat it. While he was thus having his lunch a dog almost as large as a colt came running out from the high grass. He made straight for Momotaro and, showing his teeth, said in a fierce way:

"You are a rude man to pass my field without asking permission first. If you leave me all the cakes you have in your bag you may go; otherwise I will bite you till I kill you!"

Momotaro only laughed scornfully:

"What is that you are saying? Do you know who I am? I am Momotaro, and I am on my way to subdue the devils in their island stronghold in the northeast of Japan. If you try to stop me on my way there I will cut you in two from the head downward!"

The dog's manner at once changed. His tail dropped between his legs, and coming near he bowed so low that his forehead touched the ground.

"What do I hear? The name of Momotaro? Are you indeed Momotaro? I have often heard of your great strength. Not knowing who you were I have behaved in a very stupid way. Will you please pardon my rudeness? Are you indeed on your way to invade the Island of Devils? If you will take such a rude fellow with you as one of your followers, I shall be very grateful to you."

"I think I can take you with me if you wish to go," said Momotaro.

"Thank you!" said the dog. "By the way, I am very, very hungry. Will you give me one of the cakes you are carrying?"

"This is the best kind of cake there is in Japan," said Momotaro. "I cannot spare you a whole one; I will give you half of one."

"Thank you very much," said the dog, taking the piece thrown to him.

Then Momotaro got up and the dog followed. For a long time they walked over the hills and through the valleys. As they were going along an animal came down from a tree a little ahead of them. The creature soon came up to Momotaro and said:

"Good morning, Momotaro! You are welcome in this part of the country. Will you allow me to go with you?"

The dog answered jealously:

"Momotaro already has a dog to accompany him. Of what use is a monkey like you in battle? We are on our way to fight the devils! Get away!"

The dog and the monkey began to quarrel and bite, for these two animals always hate each other.

"Now, don't quarrel!" said Momotaro, putting himself between them. "Wait a moment, dog!"

"It is not at all dignified for you to have such a creature as that following you!" said the dog.

"What do you know about it?" asked Momotaro and, pushing aside the dog, he spoke to the monkey:

"Who are you?"

"I am a monkey living in these hills," replied the monkey. "I heard of your expedition to the Island of Devils, and I have come to go with you. Nothing will please me more than to follow you!"

"Do you really wish to go to the Island of Devils and fight with me?"

"Yes, sir," replied the monkey.

"I admire your courage," said Momotaro. "Here is a piece of one of my fine rice cakes. Come along!"

So the monkey joined Momotaro. The dog and the monkey did not get on well together. They were always snapping at each other as they went along, and always wanting to have a fight. This made Momotaro very cross, and at last he sent the dog on ahead with a flag and put the monkey behind with a sword, and he placed himself between them with a war-fan, which was made of iron.

By and by they came to a large field. Here a bird flew down and alighted on the ground just in front of the little party. It was the most beautiful bird Momotaro had ever seen. On its body were five different robes of feathers and its head was covered with a scarlet cap.

The dog at once ran at the bird and tried to seize and kill it. But the bird stuck out its spurs and flew at the dog's tail, and the fight went hard with both.

Momotaro, as he looked on, could not help admiring the bird; it showed so much spirit in the fight. It would certainly make a good fighter.

Momotaro went up to the two combatants, and holding the dog back, said to the bird:

"You rascal! You are hindering my journey. Surrender at once, and I will take you with me. If you don't I will set this dog to bite your head off!"

Then the bird surrendered at once, and begged to be taken into Momotaro's company.

"I do not know what excuse to offer for quarreling with the dog, your servant, but I did not see you. I am a miserable bird called a pheasant. It is very generous of you to pardon my rudeness and to take me with you. Please allow me to follow you behind the dog and the monkey!"

"I congratulate you on surrendering so soon," said Momotaro, smiling. "Come and join us in our raid on the devils."

"Are you going to take this bird with you also?" asked the dog, interrupting.

"Why do you ask such an unnecessary question? Didn't you hear what I said? I take the bird with me because I wish to!"

"Humph!" said the dog.

Then Momotaro stood and gave this order:

"Now all of you must listen to me. The first thing necessary in an army is harmony. It is a wise saying which says that 'Advantage on earth is better than advantage in Heaven!' Union amongst ourselves is better than any earthly gain. When we are not at peace amongst ourselves it is no easy thing to subdue an enemy. From now, you three, the dog, the monkey and the pheasant, must be friends with one mind. The one who first begins a quarrel will be discharged on the spot!"

All the three promised not to quarrel. The pheasant was now made a member of Momotaro's suite, and received half a cake.

Momotaro's influence was so great that the three became good friends, and hurried onward with him as their leader.

Hurrying on day after day, they at last came out upon the shore of the North-Eastern Sea. There was nothing to be seen as

far as the horizon—not a sign of any island. All that broke the stillness was the rolling of the waves upon the shore.

Now, the dog and the monkey and the pheasant had come very bravely all the way through the long valleys and over the hills, but they had never seen the sea before, and for the first time since they set out they were bewildered and gazed at each other in silence. How were they to cross the water and get to the Island of Devils?

Momotaro soon saw that they were daunted by the sight of the sea, and to try them he spoke loudly and roughly:

"Why do you hesitate? Are you afraid of the sea? Oh! what cowards you are! It is impossible to take such weak creatures as you with me to fight the demons. It will be far better for me to go alone. I discharge you all at once!"

The three animals were taken aback at this sharp reproof, and clung to Momotaro's sleeve, begging him not to send them away.

"Please, Momotaro!" said the dog.

"We have come thus far!" said the monkey.

"It is inhuman to leave us here!" said the pheasant.

"We are not at all afraid of the sea," said the monkey again.

"Please do take us with you," said the pheasant.

"Do please," said the dog.

They had now gained a little courage, so Momotaro said:

"Well, then, I will take you with me, but be careful!"

Momotaro now got a small ship, and they all got on board. The wind and weather were fair, and the ship went like an arrow over the sea. It was the first time they had ever been on the water, and so at first the dog, the monkey and the pheasant were frightened at the waves and the rolling of the vessel, but by degrees they grew accustomed to the water and were quite happy again. Every day they paced the deck of their little ship, eagerly looking out for the demons' island.

When they grew tired of this, they told each other stories of all their exploits of which they were proud, and then played games together; and Momotaro found much to amuse him in listening to the three animals and watching their antics, and in this way he forgot that the way was long and that he was tired of the voyage and of doing nothing. He longed to be at work killing the monsters who had done so much harm in his country.

As the wind blew in their favor and they met no storms, the ship made a quick voyage, and one day when the sun was shining brightly a sight of land rewarded the four watchers at the bow.

Momotaro knew at once that what they saw was the devils' stronghold. On the top of the precipitous shore, looking out to sea, was a large castle. Now that his enterprise was close at hand, he was deep in thought, with his head leaning on his hands, wondering how he should begin the attack. His three followers watched him, waiting for orders. At last he called to the pheasant:

"It is a great advantage for us to have you with us," said Momotaro to the bird, "for you have good wings. Fly at once to the castle and engage the demons to fight. We will follow you."

The pheasant at once obeyed. He flew off from the ship, beating the air gladly with his wings. The bird soon reached the island and took up his position on the roof in the middle of the castle, calling out loudly:

"All you devils listen to me! The great Japanese general Momotaro has come to fight you and to take your stronghold from you. If you wish to save your lives surrender at once, and in token of your submission you must break off the horns that grow on your forehead. If you do not surrender at once, but make up your mind to fight, we—the pheasant, the dog and the monkey—will kill you all by biting and tearing you to death!"

The horned demons, looking up and only seeing a pheasant, laughed and said:

"A wild pheasant, indeed! It is ridiculous to hear such words from a mean thing like you. Wait till you get a blow from one of our iron bars!"

Very angry, indeed, were the devils. They shook their horns and their shocks of red hair fiercely, and rushed to put on tiger skin trousers to make themselves look more terrible. They then brought out great iron bars and ran to where the pheasant perched over their heads, and tried to knock him down. The pheasant flew to one side to escape the blow, and then attacked the head of first one and then another demon. He flew round and round them, beating the air with his wings so fiercely and ceaselessly, that the devils began to wonder whether they had to fight one or many more birds.

In the meantime, Momotaro had brought his ship to land. As they had approached, he saw that the shore was like a precipice, and that the large castle was surrounded by high walls and large iron gates and was strongly fortified.

Momotaro landed and, with the hope of finding some way of entrance, walked up the path toward the top, followed by the monkey and the dog. They soon came upon two beautiful damsels washing clothes in a stream. Momotaro saw that the clothes were bloodstained, and that as the two maidens washed, tears were falling fast down their cheeks. He stopped and spoke to them:

"Who are you, and why do you weep?"

"We are captives of the Demon King. We were carried away from our homes to this island, and though we are the daughters of Daimios [Lords], we are obliged to be his servants, and one day he will kill us"—and the maidens held up the bloodstained clothes—"and eat us, and there is no one to help us!"

And their tears burst out afresh at this horrible thought.

"I will rescue you," said Momotaro. "Do not weep any more, only show me how I may get into the castle."

Then the two ladies led the way and showed Momotaro a little back door in the lowest part of the castle wall—so small that Momotaro could hardly crawl in.

The pheasant, who was all this time fighting hard, saw Momotaro and his little band rush in at the back.

Momotaro's onslaught was so furious that the devils could not stand against him. At first their foe had been a single bird, the pheasant, but now that Momotaro and the dog and the monkey had arrived they were bewildered, for the four enemies fought like a hundred, so strong were they. Some of the devils fell off the parapet of the castle and were dashed to pieces on the rocks beneath; others fell into the sea and were drowned; many were beaten to death by the three animals.

The chief of the devils at last was the only one left. He made up his mind to surrender, for he knew that his enemy was stronger than mortal man.

He came up humbly to Momotaro and threw down his iron bar, and kneeling down at the victor's feet he broke off the horns on his head in token of submission, for they were the sign of his strength and power.

"I am afraid of you," he said meekly. "I cannot stand against you. I will give you all the treasure hidden in this castle if you will spare my life!"

Momotaro laughed.

"It is not like you, big devil, to beg for mercy, is it? I cannot spare your wicked life, however much you beg, for you have killed and tortured many people and robbed our country for many years."

Then Momotaro tied the devil chief up and gave him into the monkey's charge. Having done this, he went into all the rooms of the castle and set the prisoners free and gathered together all the treasure he found.

The dog and the pheasant carried home the plunder, and thus Momotaro returned triumphantly to his home, taking with him the devil chief as a captive.

The two poor damsels, daughters of Daimios, and others whom the wicked demon had carried off to be his slaves, were taken safely to their own homes and delivered to their parents.

The whole country made a hero of Momotaro on his triumphant return, and rejoiced that the country was now freed from the robber devils who had been a terror of the land for a long time.

The old couple's joy was greater than ever, and the treasure Momotaro had brought home with him enabled them to live in peace and plenty to the end of their days.

Salt

Once upon a time there were three brothers, and their father was a great merchant who sent his ships far over the sea, and traded here and there in countries the names of which I, being an old man, can never rightly call to mind. Well, the names of the two elder brothers do not matter, but the youngest was called Silly Ivan, because he was always playing and never working; and if there was a silly thing to do, why, off he went and did it. And so, when the brothers grew up, the father sent the two elder ones off, each in a fine ship laden with gold and jewels, and rings and bracelets, and laces and silks, and sticks with little bits of silver hammered into their handles, and spoons with patterns of blue and red, and everything else you can think of that costs too much to buy. But he made Silly Ivan stay at home, and did not give him a ship at all. Ivan saw his brothers go sailing off over the sea on a summer morning, to make their fortunes and come back rich men; and then, for the first time in his life, he wanted to work and do something useful. He went to his father and kissed his hand, and he kissed the hand of his little old mother, and he begged his father to give him a ship so that he could try his fortune like his brothers.

"But you have never done a wise thing in your life, and no one could count all the silly things you've done if he spent a hundred days in counting," said his father.

"True," said Ivan, "but now I am going to be wise, and sail the sea and come back with something in my pockets to show that I am not silly any more. Give me just a little ship, father, just a little ship for myself."

"Give him a little ship," said the mother. "He may not be silly after all."

"Very well," said his father. "I will give him a little ship, but I am not going to waste good roubles by giving him a rich cargo."

"Give me any cargo you like," said Ivan.

So his father gave him a little ship, a little old ship, and a cargo of rags and scraps and things that were not fit for anything but to be thrown away. And he gave him a crew of ancient old sailormen who were past work; and Ivan went on board and sailed away at sunset, because he was so silly. Any good seaman worth his roubles would leave at the crack of dawn. And the feeble, ancient old sailormen pulled up the ragged, dirty sails, and away they went over the sea to learn what fortune, good or bad, God had in mind for a crew of old men with a silly master.

The fourth day after they set sail, there came a great wind over the sea. The feeble old men did the best they could with the ship, but the old, torn sails tore from the masts, and the wind did what it pleased, and threw the little ship on an unknown island away in the middle of the sea. Then the wind dropped, and left the little ship on the beach, and Silly Ivan and his ancient old men, like good Russians, praising God that they were still alive.

"Well, children," said Ivan, for he knew how to talk to sailors, "you stay here and mend the sails, and make new ones out of the rags we carry as cargo, while I go inland and see if there is anything that could be of use to us."

So the ancient old sailormen sat on deck with their legs crossed, and made sails out of rags, of torn scraps of old brocades, of soiled embroidered shawls, of all the rubbish that they had with

them for a cargo. You never saw such sails. The tide came up and
floated the ship, and they threw out anchors at bow and stern, and
sat there in the sunlight, making sails and patching them and
talking of the days when they were young. All this while Silly Ivan
went walking off into the island.

Now in the middle of that island was a high mountain, a high
mountain it was, and so white that when he came near it Silly Ivan
began thinking of sheepskin coats, although it was midsummer
and the sun was hot in the sky. The trees were green round about,
but there was nothing growing on the mountain at all. It was just
a great white mountain piled up into the sky in the middle of a
green island. Ivan walked a little way up the white slopes of the
mountain, and then, because he felt thirsty, he thought he would
let a little snow melt in his mouth. He took some in his fingers and
stuffed it in. Quickly enough, it came out again, I can tell you, for
the mountain was not made of snow but of good Russian salt.
And you know what a mouthful of salt is like!

Silly Ivan did not stop to think twice. The salt was so clean and
shone so brightly in the sunlight. He just turned round and ran
back to the shore, and called out to his ancient old sailormen and
told them to empty everything they had on board over into the sea.
Over it all went, rags and tags and rotten timbers, till the little ship
was as empty as a soup bowl after supper. And then those ancient
old men were set to work carrying salt from the mountain and
taking it on board the little ship, and stowing it away below deck
till there was not room for another grain. Silly Ivan would have
liked to take the whole mountain, but there was not room in the
little ship. And for that the ancient old sailormen thanked God,
because their backs ached and their old legs were weak, and they
said they would have died if they had had to carry any more.

Then they hoisted up the new sails they had patched together
out of the rags and scraps of shawls and old brocades, and they

sailed away once more over the blue sea. And the wind stood fair, and they sailed before it, and the ancient old sailors tested their backs, and told old tales, and took turns at the rudder.

And after many days' sailing they came to a town, with towers and churches and painted roofs, all set on the side of a hill that sloped down into the sea. At the foot of the hill was a quiet harbor, and they sailed in there and moored the ship and hauled down their patchwork sails.

Silly Ivan went ashore, and took with him a little bag of clean white salt to show what kind of goods he had for sale, and he asked his way to the palace of the Tzar of that town. He came to the palace, and went in and bowed to the ground before the Tzar.

"Who are you?" asked the Tzar.

"I, great lord, am a Russian merchant, and here in a bag is some of my merchandise, and I beg your leave to trade with your subjects in this town."

"Let me see what is in the bag," said the Tzar.

Silly Ivan took a handful from the bag and showed it to the Tzar.

"What is it?" asked the Tzar.

"Good Russian salt," replied Silly Ivan.

Now in that country they had never heard of salt, and the Tzar looked at the salt, and he looked at Ivan and he laughed.

"Why, this," said he, "is nothing but white dust, and that we can pick up for nothing. The men of my town have no need to trade with you. You must be silly."

Ivan grew very red, for he knew what his father used to call him. He was ashamed to say anything. So he bowed to the ground, and went away out of the palace.

But when he was outside he thought to himself, "I wonder what sort of salt they use in these parts if they do not know good Russian salt when they see it. I will go to the kitchen."

So he went round to the back door of the palace, and put his head into the kitchen, and said, "I am very tired. May I sit down here and rest a little while?"

"Come in," said one of the cooks. "But you must sit just there and not put even your little finger in the way of us; for we are the Tzar's cooks, and we are in the middle of making ready his dinner." And the cook put a stool in a corner out of the way, and Ivan slipped in round the door, and sat down in the corner and looked about him. There were seven cooks at least, boiling and baking, and stewing and toasting, and roasting and frying. And as for scullions, they were as thick as cockroaches, dozens of them, running to and fro, tumbling over each other, and helping the cooks.

Silly Ivan sat on his stool, with his legs tucked under him and the bag of salt on his knees. He watched the cooks and the scullions, but he did not see them put anything in the dishes that he thought could take the place of salt. No; the meat was without salt, the kasha was without salt, and there was no salt in the potatoes. Ivan nearly turned sick at the thought of the tastelessness of all that food.

There came the moment when all the cooks and scullions ran out of the kitchen to fetch the silver platters on which to lay the dishes. Ivan slipped down from his stool, and running from stove to stove, from saucepan to frying pan, he dropped a pinch of salt, just what was wanted, no more, no less, in every one of the dishes. Then he ran back to the stool in the corner, and sat there, and watched the dishes being put on the silver platters and carried off in gold-embroidered napkins to be the dinner of the Tzar.

The Tzar sat at table and took his first spoonful of soup.

"The soup is very good today," said he, and he finished the soup to the last drop.

"I've never known the soup so good," said the Tzaritza, and she finished hers.

"This is the best soup I ever tasted," said the Princess, and down went hers, and she, you know, was the prettiest princess who ever had dinner in this world.

It was the same with the kasha and the same with the meat. The Tzar and the Tzaritza and the Princess wondered why they had never had so good a dinner in all their lives before.

"Call the cooks," ordered the Tzar. And they called the cooks, and the cooks all came in, and bowed to the ground, and stood in a row before the Tzar.

"What did you put in the dishes today that you never put before?" asked the Tzar.

"We put nothing unusual, your greatness," replied the cooks, and bowed to the ground again.

"Then why do the dishes taste better?"

"We do not know, your greatness," said the cooks.

"Call the scullions," said the Tzar. And the scullions were

called, and they too bowed to the ground, and stood in a row before the Tzar.

"What was done in the kitchen today that has not been done there before?" asked the Tzar.

"Nothing, your greatness," said all the scullions except one.

And that one scullion bowed again, and kept on bowing, and then he said, "Please, your greatness, please, great lord, there is usually no one in the kitchen but ourselves; but today there was a young Russian merchant, who sat on a stool in the corner and said he was tired."

"Call the merchant," said the Tzar.

So they brought in Silly Ivan, and he bowed before the Tzar, and stood there with his little bag of salt in his hand.

"Did you do anything to my dinner?" asked the Tzar.

"I did, your greatness," said Ivan.

"What did you do?"

"I put a pinch of Russian salt in every dish."

"That white dust?" said the Tzar.

"Nothing but that."

"Have you got any more of it?"

"I have a little ship in the harbor laden with nothing else," said Ivan.

"It is the most wonderful dust in the world," said the Tzar, "and I will buy every grain of it you have. What do you want for it?"

Silly Ivan scratched his head and thought. He thought that if the Tzar liked it as much as all that it must be worth a fair price, so he said, "We will put the salt into bags, and for every bag of salt you must give me three bags of the same weight—one of gold, one of silver, and one of precious stones. Cheaper than that, your greatness, I could not possibly sell."

"Agreed," said the Tzar. "And a cheap price, too, for a dust so full of magic that it makes dull dishes tasty, and tasty dishes so good that there is no looking away from them."

So all the day long, and far into the night, the ancient old sailormen bent their backs under sacks of salt, and bent them again under sacks of gold and silver and precious stones. When all the salt had been put in the Tzar's treasury—yes, with twenty soldiers guarding it with great swords shining in the moonlight— and when the little ship was loaded with riches, so that even the deck was piled high with precious stones, the ancient old men lay down among the jewels and slept till morning, when Silly Ivan went to bid goodbye to the Tzar.

"And whither shall you sail now?" asked the Tzar.

"I shall sail away to Russia in my little ship," replied Ivan.

And the Princess, who was very beautiful, said, "A little Russian ship?"

"Yes," said Ivan.

"I have never seen a Russian ship," said the Princess, and she begged her father to let her go to the harbor with her nurses and maids, to see the little Russian ship before Ivan set sail.

She came with Ivan to the harbor, and the ancient old sailormen took them on board.

She ran all over the ship, looking now at this and now at that, and Ivan told her the names of everything: deck, mast, and rudder.

"May I see the sails?" she asked. And the ancient old men hoisted the ragged sails, and the wind filled the sails and tugged.

"Why doesn't the ship move when the sails are up?" asked the Princess.

"The anchor holds her," said Ivan.

"Please let me see the anchor," said the Princess.

"Haul up the anchor, my children, and show it to the Princess," said Ivan to the ancient old sailormen.

And the old men hauled up the anchor, and showed it to the Princess; and she said it was a very good little anchor. But, of course, as soon as the anchor was up the ship began to move. One

of the ancient old men bent over the tiller, and, with a fair wind behind her, the little ship slipped out of the harbor and away to the blue sea. When the Princess looked round, thinking it was time to go home, the little ship was far from land, and away in the distance she could only see the gold towers of her father's palace, glittering like pinpoints in the sunlight. Her nurses and maids wrung their hands and cried out, and the Princess sat down on a heap of jewels, and put a handkerchief to her eyes, and cried and cried and cried.

Silly Ivan took her hands and comforted her, and told her of the wonders of the sea that he would show her, and the wonders of the land. And she looked up at him while he talked, and his eyes were kind and hers were sweet; and the end of it was that they were both very well content, and agreed to have a marriage feast as soon as the little ship should bring them to the home of Ivan's father. Merry was that voyage. All day long Ivan and the Princess sat on deck and said sweet things to each other, and at twilight they sang songs, and drank tea, and told stories. As for the nurses and maids, the Princess told them to be glad; and so they danced and clapped their hands, and ran about the ship, and teased the ancient old sailormen.

When they had been sailing many days, the Princess was looking out over the sea, and she cried out to Ivan, "See, over there, far away, are two big ships with white sails, not like our sails of brocade and bits of silk."

Ivan looked, shading his eyes with his hands.

"Why, those are the ships of my elder brothers," said he. "We shall all sail home together."

And he made the ancient old sailormen give a hail in their cracked old voices. And the brothers heard them, and came on board to greet Ivan and his bride. When they saw that she was a Tzar's daughter, and that the very decks were heaped with

precious stones, because there was no room below, they said one thing to Ivan and something else to each other.

To Ivan they said, "Thanks be to God, He has given you good trading."

But to each other, "How can this be?" said one. "Silly Ivan is bringing back such a cargo, while we in our fine ships have only a bag or two of gold."

"And what is Silly Ivan doing with a princess?" said the other.

And they ground their teeth, and waited their time, and when Ivan was alone in the twilight, they came up suddenly, and picked him up by his head and his heels, and threw him overboard into the dark blue sea.

Not one of the old men had seen them, and the Princess was not on deck. In the morning they said that Silly Ivan must have walked overboard in sleep. And they drew lots. The eldest brother took the Princess, and the second brother took the little ship laden with gold and silver and precious stones. And so the brothers sailed home very well content. But the Princess sat and wept all day long, looking down into the blue water. The elder brother could not comfort her, and the second brother did not try. And the ancient old sailormen muttered in their beards, and were sorry, and prayed to God to give rest to Ivan's soul; for although he was silly, and although he had made them carry a lot of salt and other things, yet they loved him, because he knew how to talk to ancient old sailormen.

But Ivan was not dead. As soon as he splashed into the water, he crammed his fur hat a little tighter on his head, and began swimming in the sea. He swam about until the sun rose, and then, not far away, he saw a floating timber log, and he swam to the log, and got astride of it, and thanked God. And he sat there on the log in the middle of the sea, twiddling his thumbs for want of something to do.

There was a strong current in the sea that carried him along, and at last, after floating for many days without ever a bite for his teeth or a drop for his gullet, one night his feet touched land. He left the log and walked up out of the sea, and lay down on the shore and waited for morning.

When the sun rose he stood up, and saw that he was on a bare island, and he saw nothing at all on the island except a huge house as big as a mountain; and as he was looking at the house the great door creaked with a noise like that of a hurricane among the pine forests, and opened; and a giant came walking out, and came to the shore, and stood there, looking down at Ivan.

"What are you doing here, little one?" asked the giant.

Ivan told him the whole story, just as I have told it to you.

The giant listened to the very end, pulling at his monstrous whiskers. Then he said, "Listen, little one. I know more of the story than you, for I can tell you that tomorrow morning your eldest brother is going to marry your Princess. But there is no need for you to worry about it. If you want to be there, I will carry you and set you down before the house in time for the wedding. And a fine wedding it will be, for your father thinks well of those brothers of yours bringing back all those precious stones, and silver and gold enough to buy a kingdom."

And with that he picked up Silly Ivan and set him on his great shoulders, and set off striding through the sea.

He went so fast that the wind blew off Ivan's hat.

"Stop a moment," shouted Ivan, "my hat has blown off."

"We can't turn back for that," said the giant, "we have already left your hat far behind us." And he rushed on, splashing through the sea. The sea was up to his armpits. He rushed on, and the sea was up to his waist. He rushed on, and before the sun had climbed to the top of the blue sky he was splashing up out of the sea with the water about his ankles. He lifted Ivan from his shoulders and set him on the ground.

"Now," said he, "little man, off you run, and you'll be in time for the feast. But don't you dare to boast about riding on my shoulders. If you open your mouth about that you'll be sorry, even if I have to come from the ends of the earth."

Silly Ivan thanked the giant for carrying him through the sea, promised that he would not boast, and then ran off to his father's house. Long before he got there, he heard the musicians in the courtyard playing as if they wanted to wear out their instruments before night. The wedding feast had begun, and when Ivan ran in, there, at the high board, was sitting the Princess, and beside her his eldest brother. And there were his father and mother, his second brother, and all the guests. And every one of them was as merry as could be, except the Princess, and she was as white as the salt he had sold to her father.

Suddenly the blood flushed into her checks. She saw Ivan in the doorway. Up she jumped at the high board, and cried out,

"There, there is my true love, and not this man who sits beside me at the table."

"What is this?" demanded Ivan's father, and in a few minutes knew the whole story.

He turned the two elder brothers out of doors, gave their ships to Ivan, married him to the Princess, and made him his heir. The wedding feast began again, and they sent for the ancient old sailormen to take part in it. And the ancient old sailormen wept with joy when they saw Ivan and the Princess, like two sweet pigeons, sitting side by side; yes, and they lifted their flagons with their old shaking hands, and cheered with their old cracked voices, and poured the wine down their dry old throats.

There was wine enough and to spare, beer too, and mead, enough to drown a herd of cattle. And as the guests drank and grew merry and proud, they set to boasting. This one bragged of his riches, that one of his wife. Another boasted of his cunning, another of his new house, another of his strength, and this one was angry because they would not let him show how he could lift the table on one hand. They all drank to Ivan's health, and he drank to theirs, and in the end he could not bear to listen to their proud boasts.

"That's all very well," said he, "but I am the only man in the world who rode on the shoulders of a giant to come to his wedding feast."

The words were scarcely out of his mouth before there were a tremendous trampling and a roar of a great wind. The house shook with the footsteps of the giant as he strode up. The giant bent down over the courtyard and looked in at the feast.

"Little man, little man," said he, "you promised not to boast of me. I told you what would come if you did, and here you are and have boasted already."

"Forgive me," said Ivan. "It was the drink that boasted, not I."

"What sort of drink is it that knows how to boast?" asked the giant.

"You shall taste it," said Ivan.

And he made his ancient old sailormen roll a great barrel of wine into the yard, more than enough for a hundred men, and after that a barrel of beer that was as big, and then a barrel of mead that was no smaller.

"Try the taste of that," said Silly Ivan.

Well, the giant did not wait to be asked twice. He lifted the barrel of wine as if it had been a little glass, and emptied it down his throat. He lifted the barrel of beer as if it had been an acorn, and emptied it after the wine. Then he lifted the barrel of mead as if it had been a very small pea, and swallowed every drop of mead that was in it. And after that he began stamping about and breaking things. Houses fell to pieces this way and that, and trees were swept flat like grass. Every step the giant took was followed

by the crash of breaking timbers. Then suddenly he fell flat on his back and slept. For three days and nights he slept without waking. At last he opened his eyes.

"Just look about you," said Ivan, "and see the damage that you've done."

"And did that little drop of drink make me do all that?" said the giant. "Well, well, I can well understand that a drink like that can do a bit of bragging. And after that," said he, looking at the wrecks of houses, and all the broken things scattered about—"after that," said he, "you can boast of me for a thousand years, and I'll have nothing against you."

And he tugged at his great whiskers, and wrinkled his eyes, and went striding off into the sea.

That is the story about salt, and how it made a rich man of Silly Ivan, and besides, gave him the prettiest wife in the world, and she is a Tzar's daughter.

Chelm Justice

JEWISH

A great calamity befell Chelm one day. The town cobbler murdered one of his customers. So he was brought before the judge, who sentenced him to die by hanging. When the verdict was read a townsman arose and cried out, "If Your Honor pleases—you have sentenced to death the town cobbler! He's the only one we've got. If you hang him who will mend our shoes?"

"Who? Who?" cried all the people of Chelm with one voice.

The judge nodded in agreement and reconsidered his verdict.

"Good people of Chelm," he said, "What you say is true. Since we have only one cobbler it would be a great wrong against the community to let him die. As there are two roofers in the town, let one of them be hanged instead!"

Sadko

RUSSIA

In Novgorod in the old days there was a young man—just a
boy he was—the son of a rich merchant who had lost all his
money and died. So Sadko was very poor. He had not a
kopeck in the world, except what the people gave him when he
played his dulcimer for their dancing. He had blue eyes and
curling hair, and he was strong, and would have been merry. But
it is dull work playing for other folk to dance, and Sadko dared not
dance with any young girl, for he had no money to marry on, and
he did not want to be chased away as a beggar. And the young
women of Novgorod never looked at the handsome Sadko. No;
they smiled with their bright eyes at the young men who danced
with them, and if they ever spoke to Sadko, it was just to tell him
sharply to keep the music going or to play faster.

So Sadko lived alone with his dulcimer and made do with half
a loaf when he could not get a whole, and with crust when he had
no crumb. He did not mind so very much what came to him, so
long as he could play his dulcimer and walk along the bank of the
river Volkhov that flows by Novgorod, or on the shore of the lake,
making music for himself, and seeing the pale mists rise over the
water, and dawn or sunset across the shining river.

"There is no girl in all Novgorod as pretty as my little river," he
used to say, and night after night he would sit by the banks of the

river or on the shores of the lake, playing the dulcimer and singing to himself.

Sometimes he helped the fishermen on the lake, and they would give him a little fish for his supper in payment for his strong young arms.

And it happened that one evening the fishermen asked him to watch their nets for them on the shore, while they went off to sell their fish in the square at Novgorod.

Sadko sat on the shore, on a rock, and played his dulcimer and sang. Very sweetly he sang of the fair lake and the lovely river: the one that he thought prettier than all the girls of Novgorod. And while he was singing he saw a whirlpool in the lake, little waves flying from it across the water, and in the middle a hollow down into the water. And in the hollow he saw the head of a great man with blue hair and a gold crown. He knew that the huge man was the Tzar of the Sea. And the man came nearer, walking up out of the depths of the lake—a huge, great man, a very giant, with blue hair falling to his waist over his broad shoulders. The little waves ran from him in all directions as he came striding up out of the water.

Sadko did not know whether to run or stay; but the Tzar of the Sea called out to him in a great voice like wind and water in a storm:

"Sadko of Novgorod, you have played and sung many days by the side of this lake and on the bank of the little river Volkhov. My daughters love your music, and it has pleased me too. Throw out a net into the water, and draw it in, and the waters will pay you for your singing. And if you are satisfied with the payment, you must come and play to us down in the green palace of the sea."

With that the Tzar of the Sea went down again into the waters of the lake. The waves closed over him with a roar, and presently the lake was as smooth and calm as it had ever been.

Sadko said to himself: "Well, there is no harm done in casting out a net." So he threw a net out into the lake.

He sat down again and played on his dulcimer and sang, and when he had finished his singing the dusk had fallen and the moon shone over the lake. He put down his dulcimer and took hold of the ropes of the net, and began to draw it up out of the silver water. Easily the ropes came, and the net dripped and glittered in the moonlight.

"I was dreaming," said Sadko. "I was asleep when I saw the Tzar of the Sea, and there is nothing in the net at all."

And then, just as the last of the net was coming ashore, he saw something in it, square and dark. He dragged it out and found it was a coffer. He opened the coffer, and it was full of precious stones—green, red, gold—gleaming in the light of the moon. Diamonds shone there like little bundles of sharp knives.

"There can be no harm in taking these stones," said Sadko, "whether I dreamed or not."

He took the coffer on his shoulder, and bent under the weight of it, strong though he was. He put it in a safe place. All night he sat and watched by the nets, and played, and sang, and planned what he would do.

In the morning the fishermen came, laughing and merry after their night in Novgorod, and they gave him a little fish for watching their nets. Sadko made a fire on the shore, and cooked the fish and ate it as he used to do.

"And that is my last meal as a poor man," said Sadko. "Ah me! who knows if I shall be happier?"

Then he set the coffer on his shoulder and tramped away for Novgorod.

"Who is that?" they asked at the gates.

"Only Sadko the dulcimer player," he replied.

"Turned porter?" said they.

"One trade is as good as another," said Sadko, and he walked into the city. He sold a few of the stones, two at a time, and with what he got for them he set up a booth in the market. Small things led to great, and he was soon one of the richest traders in Novgorod.

And now there was not a girl in the town who could look too sweetly at Sadko. "He has golden hair," said one. "Blue eyes like the sea," said another. "He could lift the world on his shoulders," said a third. A little money, you see, opens everybody's eyes.

But Sadko was not changed by his good fortune. Still he walked and played by the little river Volkhov. When work was done and the traders gone, Sadko would take his dulcimer and play and sing on the bank of the river. And still he said, "There is no girl in all Novgorod as pretty as my little river." Every time he came back from his long voyages—for he was trading far and near, like the greatest of merchants—he went at once to the bank of the river to see how his sweetheart fared. And always he brought some little present for her and threw it into the waves.

For twelve years he lived unmarried in Novgorod, and every year made voyages, buying and selling, and always growing richer and richer. Many were the mothers in Novgorod who would have liked to see him married to their daughters. Many were the pillows that were wet with the tears of the young girls, as they thought of the blue eyes of Sadko and his golden hair.

And then, in the twelfth year since he walked into Novgorod with the coffer on his shoulder, he was sailing in a ship on the Caspian Sea, far, far away. For many days the ship sailed on, and Sadko sat on deck and played his dulcimer and sang of Novgorod and of the little river Volkhov that flows under the walls of the town. Blue was the Caspian Sea, and the waves were like furrows

in a field, long lines of white under the steady wind, while the sails swelled and the ship shot over the water.

And suddenly the ship stopped.

In the middle of the sea, far from land, the ship stopped and trembled in the waves, as if she were held by a big hand.

"We are aground!" cried the sailors; and the captain, the great one, told them to take soundings. Seventy fathoms by the bow it was, and seventy fathoms by the stern.

"We are not aground," said the captain, "unless there is a rock sticking up like a needle in the middle of the Caspian Sea!"

"There is magic in this," said the sailors.

"Hoist more sail," ordered the captain; and up went the white sails, swelling out in the wind, while the masts bent and creaked.

But still the ship lay shivering and did not move, out there in the middle of the sea.

"Hoist more sail yet," said the captain; and up went the white sails, swelling and tugging, while the masts creaked and groaned. But still the ship lay there shivering and did not move.

"There is an unlucky one aboard," said an old sailor. "We must draw lots and find him, and throw him overboard into the sea."

The other sailors agreed to this. And still Sadko sat, and played his dulcimer and sang.

The sailors cut pieces of string, all of a length, as many as there were souls in the ship, and one of those strings they cut in half. Then they made them into a bundle, and each man plucked one string. And Sadko stopped his playing for a moment to pluck a string, and his was the string that had been cut in half.

"Magician, sorcerer, unclean one!" shouted the sailors.

"Not so," said Sadko. "I remember now an old promise I made, and I keep it willingly."

He took his dulcimer in his hand, and leapt from the ship into the blue Caspian Sea. The waves had scarcely closed over his head before the ship shot forward again, and flew over the waves like a swan's feather, and came in the end safely to her harbor.

Sadko dropped into the waves, and the waves closed over him. Down he sank, like a pebble thrown into a pool, down and down. First the water blue, then green, and strange fish with goggle eyes and golden fins swam round him as he sank. He came at last to the bottom of the sea.

And there, on the bottom of the sea, was a palace built of green wood. Yes, all the timbers of all the ships that had been wrecked in all the seas of the world were in that palace, and they were all green, and cunningly fitted together, so that the palace was worth a ten days' journey to see it. And in front of the palace Sadko saw two big knobbly sturgeons, each a hundred and fifty feet long, lashing

their tails and guarding the gates. Now, sturgeons are the oldest of all fish, and these were the oldest of all sturgeons.

Sadko walked between the sturgeons and through the gates of the palace. Inside there was a great hall, and the Tzar of the Sea lay resting in the hall, with his gold crown on his head and his blue hair floating round him in the water, and his great body covered with scales lying along the hall. The Tzar of the Sea filled the hall, and there was room in that hall for a village. And there were fish swimming this way and that, in and out of the windows.

"Ah, Sadko," said the Tzar of the Sea, "you took what the sea gave you, but you have been a long time in coming to sing in the palaces of the sea. Twelve years I have lain here waiting for you."

"Great Tzar, forgive me," says Sadko.

"Sing now," said the Tzar of the Sea, and his voice was like the beating of waves.

And Sadko played on his dulcimer and sang.

He sang of Novgorod and of the little river Volkhov which he loved. It was in his song that none of the girls of Novgorod were as pretty as the little river. And there was the sound of wind over the lake in his song, the sound of ripples under the prow of a boat, the sound of ripples on the shore, the sound of the river flowing past the tall reeds, the whispering sound of the river at night. And all the time he played cunningly on the dulcimer. The girls of Novgorod had never danced to so sweet a tune when in the old days Sadko played his dulcimer to earn kopecks and crusts of bread.

Never had the Tzar of the Sea heard such music.

"I would dance," said the Tzar of the Sea, and he stood up like a tall tree in the hall.

"Play on," said the Tzar of the Sea, and he strode through the gates. The sturgeons guarding the gates stirred the water with their tails.

And if the Tzar of the Sea was huge in the hall, he was huger still when he stood outside on the bottom of the sea. He grew taller and taller, towering like a mountain. His feet were like small hills. His blue hair hung down to his waist, and he was covered with green scales. And he began to dance on the bottom of the sea.

Great was that dancing. The sea boiled, and ships went down. The waves rolled as big as houses. The sea overflowed its shores, and whole towns were under water as the Tzar danced mightily on the bottom of the sea. Hither and thither rushed the waves, and the very earth shook at the dancing of that tremendous Tzar.

He danced till he was tired, and then he came back to the palace of green wood, and passed the sturgeons, and shrank into himself and came through the gates into the hall, where Sadko still played on his dulcimer and sang.

"You have played well and given me pleasure," said the Tzar of the Sea. "I have thirty daughters, and you shall choose one and marry her, and be a Prince of the Sea."

"Better than all maidens I love my little river," said Sadko, and the Tzar of the Sea laughed and threw his head back, with his blue hair floating all over the hall.

And then there came in the thirty daughters of the Tzar of the Sea. Beautiful they were, lovely, and graceful; but twenty-nine of them passed by, and Sadko fingered his dulcimer and thought of his little river.

There came in the thirtieth, and Sadko cried out aloud. "Here is the only maiden in the world as pretty as my little river!" said he. And she looked at him with eyes that shone like stars reflected in the river. Her hair was dark, like the river at night. She laughed, and her voice was like the flowing of the river.

"And what is the name of your little river?" said the Tzar.

"It is the little river Volkhov that flows by Novgorod," said Sadko, "but your daughter is as fair as the little river, and I would gladly marry her if she will have me."

"It is a strange thing," said the Tzar, "but Volkhov is the name of my youngest daughter."

He put Sadko's hand in the hand of his youngest daughter, and

they kissed each other. And as they kissed, Sadko saw a necklace round her neck, and knew it for one he had thrown into the river as a present for his sweetheart.

She smiled, and "Come!" said she, and took him away to a palace of her own, and showed him a coffer; and in that coffer were bracelets and rings and earrings, all the gifts that he had thrown into the river.

And Sadko laughed for joy, and kissed the youngest daughter of the Tzar of the Sea, and she kissed him back.

"O my little river!" said he. "There is no girl in all the world who is as pretty as my little river."

Well, they were married, and the Tzar of the Sea laughed at the wedding feast till the palace shook and the fish swam off in all directions.

And after the feast Sadko and his bride went off together to her palace. And before they slept she kissed him very tenderly, and she said:

"O Sadko, you will not forget me? You will play to me sometimes, and sing?"

"I shall never lose sight of you, my pretty one," said he, "and as for music, I will sing and play all the day long."

"That's as may be," said she, and they fell asleep.

And in the middle of the night Sadko happened to turn in bed, and he touched the Princess with his left foot, and she was cold, cold, cold as ice in January. And with that touch of cold he woke, and he was lying under the walls of Novgorod, with his dulcimer in his hand, and one of his feet was in the little river Volkhov, and the moon was shining.

Sadko took his dulcimer and swam out into the middle of the river, and sank under water again, looking for his little princess. He found her, and lives still in the green palaces of the bottom of the sea. When there is a big storm, you may know that Sadko is playing on his dulcimer and singing, and that the Tzar of the Sea is dancing his tremendous dance down there on the bottom, under the waves.

Those Stubborn Souls, the Biellese

ITALY

A farmer was on his way to Biella. The weather was bad, but he had important business. An old man said to him, "Good day! Where are you going?"

"To Biella," answered the farmer, without slowing down.

"You might at least say, 'God willing.'"

"God willing, I'm to Biella, but even if God isn't, I still have to go."

Now the old man happened to be the Lord and said, "In that case you'll jump into this swamp and stay for seven years."

The farmer changed into a frog and jumped into the swamp.

Seven years went by and the farmer came out of the swamp. He turned back into a man and continued to market.

After a while, he met the old man again. "And where are you going, good man?"

"To Biella."

"You might say, 'God willing.'"

"If God wills it, fine. If not, then I know what to do and can jump into the swamp without any help."

The People from Schwarzenborn

GERMANY

They Hide a Bell

❖ There are many stories about the silly actions of the people from Schwarzenborn. Once, for instance, the people from Schwarzenborn wanted to put their bell in a safe place. There probably was a war, and bells were being gathered. They took the bell to a nearby lake and put it into a boat.

Then they deliberated. "Well, if we let the bell down, then nobody will know where it is. We must have a sign to lead us."

Suddenly one of them had a good idea. "We will make a notch in the boat in the place where we drop the bell!"

They Sow Salt

❖ There was a time when salt was scarce. The people from Schwarzenborn said, "We are going to sow salt. We have still a few pounds left. If we sow these, we will have our own salt."

This was what they did. The salt came up nicely, and they were very pleased. But it was all stinging nettles.

Once they decided to see how it was growing. They went with their bare feet into the field, and it stung so much that they cried, "Oh, our salt is sharp. It is going to be sharp!"

They Protect Their Seed

❖ One day a man came to the mayor of Schwarzenborn and said that there was a cow in a field and how were they to get it out again.

The mayor said, "Well, let us see what can be done about it. We must send someone to chase the cow away."

"Yes, but he will trample everything down."

"Well, in that case, two men will have to carry the one, and he must take the shovel and drive out that cow."

They Dig a Well

❖ The people from Schwarzenborn once wanted to dig a well, but they did not know what to do with the earth they brought to the surface. At last the town council took care of the matter and decided that they should dig another hole and put the earth in there. One of the town councilors who thought he was cleverer than the others asked what should be done with the earth from this new hole. The mayor said, "What a silly question! The new hole must, of course, be big enough to hold both heaps of earth."

They Measure the Depth of the Well

❖ When the well was finished, the people from Schwarzenborn wanted to know how deep it was. As they had no metric measure, they soon contrived a very ingenious means to fathom the pit. They placed a bar across the well, and one of them clung to it, grasping the bar with both hands and dangling his legs into the well. A second one clung to his legs, a third one to the second one's legs, and so on until it grew too heavy for the first one.

"Hold on. I have to spit on my hands!" he shouted to the others.

He let go of the bar, and they all fell into the well.

The Parish Bull Eats the Grass from the Wall

❖ When the old church with its steeple and wall was still standing, grass grew on the wall and the people from Kastenholz were sorry that this grass was going to waste. So they took the parish bull and led him to the wall. Because the wall was too high, they had to draw him up so that he could eat the grass.

259

While they were pulling, the bull stretched his tongue out, and they shouted, "Look, he is stretching his tongue toward the grass!" However, they had strangled him, and that is why he stretched his tongue out.

Stretching the Bench

❖ A man in Mutschingen had a bench, and on this bench six men used to sit, deliberating what they were going to do during the week. In winter when it was cold, they would wear their furs and thus there was only room for five of them. They thought the bench had shrunk.

They said, "Come on. Let's stretch the bench. It's shrunk!"

They seized it and pulled; in doing so they got so warm that they began to sweat. They took their coats off. Then they went on stretching for a while, and at length sat down quickly; now there was room for six again. After a while, however, they felt cold and put on their furs again. And again there was only room for five of them. So they had to stretch again, and they did this the whole day.

Moving the Church

❖ The church was not standing in the proper place. In the opinion of the city fathers, it had to be pushed back a little. So they started pushing. One of them became especially warm. He took his coat off and placed it behind the church, on the very spot to which the church was being moved. A traveling journeyman came along, took the coat, and disappeared. When the owner of the garment looked for it, he believed, and so did the other city fathers, that they had pushed the church over the coat. They were very pleased with the success of their effort.

Why Wolves Chase Deer

TSIMSHIAN, NATIVE NORTH AMERICAN

One day the wolves met in a forest clearing to sing and boast about their adventures. The cubs joined in and the howling filled the valley.

The howling was so loud, other creatures fled. Only the moon liked the singing. She came out to walk among the tree tops and stood listening for most of the night.

The mists carried the wolves' voices through the forest. The deer were curious, and came to see who these creatures were. They thought the howling strange and didn't believe the tales. They started to whisper, then snigger and laugh.

The wolves were not pleased. They glared at the deer who couldn't stop laughing. If only they had. But they were bigger than the wolves and had no fear.

The wolves saw that the deer's laughing mouths had no fangs in them. Realizing that the large deer could not defend themselves they surged across the river. The deer fled.

To this day the deer are running and the wolves follow.

The Flea

This is the story of a rich landowner who loved to laugh. This rich landowner loved a good joke but best of all he loved riddles no one could answer. One day, after a dusty ride across his land, the rich landowner was tired but still in a good mood. As one of his workers helped him remove his riding jacket, a flea jumped and landed on top of the landowner's nose. Putting his hands up, the rich landowner captured the flea with one swift gesture.

He smiled, for now he had a wonderful idea. He told his worker to fetch him the *mayordomo*, the landowner's steward, and to tell him it was urgent. The worker ran, and returned with the *mayordomo*.

Taking the *mayordomo* into his study, the landowner spoke with him privately. Then he put the tiny flea in the *mayordomo*'s hand.

"I want you to feed this flea until it is the size of a cow. Do not tell anyone what it is. If anyone finds out, you will lose your life. Now go, and come back to me when that flea is the size of a cow." The *mayordomo* nodded and left the rich landowner chuckling to himself.

Well. You can be sure that the *mayordomo* did not tell anyone about this flea. Not only was he embarrassed at the silliness of this idea but he could not afford to lose his life. He had a wife and seven children, and his job paid well.

It was some time after this that the rich landowner's wife gave birth to a beautiful girl. Shortly after, the landowner's wife died, leaving the landowner alone to raise his daughter. She grew quickly and well, and learned to love laughing as much as her father. Soon it was her fourteenth birthday, and many young men came to court her. Her father was strict and sent the young men away.

One day the *mayordomo* came to speak with the rich landowner. "What brings you here, my good man?" The *mayordomo* reminded the rich landowner of the flea.

The landowner laughed. "Oh yes, I remember. Is it as big as a cow?"

The *mayordomo* shook his head. "No," he said, "but it is as big as a small calf. But the flea is now old and I fear it will soon die."

"Very good," said the landowner. "Now wait until dark and bring the flea to the barn. Make sure no one sees you, or else!"

That night the rich landowner laid his eyes for the second time on the flea. The flea could barely breathe, it was so old and fat. The landowner patted it and said, "Goodbye, flea. Your life will not be wasted. You will be put to good use."

The flea died later that night, and then the rich landowner and the *mayordomo* skinned it. The landowner then rode his best horse out into the night. He rode to a small town far to the north, to the home of an old Indian drum maker. The old Indian welcomed the landowner. They spoke into the night and then the landowner rode home.

Three weeks passed and the landowner once again saddled his horse and rode to the old Indian. The old Indian handed the landowner a perfectly round tambourine, which he kept hidden until his daughter's sixteenth birthday. On that day he gave it to her, and told her it would be the riddle that must be answered if she were ever to be married.

The daughter invited all her friends to a birthday party, and she danced with her new tambourine. When she finished, her father clapped his hands.

"Whoever can tell me what this tambourine is made of may marry my daughter." The landowner's eyes sparkled mischeviously.

Many of the young men ran and, kneeling, told him it was made from goatskin, or calfskin, or sheepskin. The landowner only laughed and laughed. They were all wrong.

The riddle lasted a very long time—well into the daughter's seventeenth year. But the landowner had now tired of the riddle and of the young men who tried to answer it. He decided that anyone who did not answer correctly would be horsewhipped. That way he would no longer be bothered with suitors. It worked. Very few came to try.

Now, the story goes that up in the hills there lived a sheepherder and his family. The youngest of the boys heard of this riddle, and thought that if only he answered it he would have money and a beautiful wife. He was tired of eating last and being blamed for the lost sheep.

So, with half a tortilla in his pocket, he decided to try his luck.

Now, this young sheepherder had spent most of his life walking up and down mountains. So he had a difficult time walking on the flat path to the rich landowner's home. He kept tripping and falling flat. At one point he fell on an ant hill. He lifted his head, and before him was a large red ant ready to sting him.

The sheepherder said, "Oh, please, I fell by accident. I mean no harm."

The ant replied, "All right. But just for that, I'd like you to carry me to town. I'm curious to see it."

The sheepherder said, "Well, I am going to the rich landowner's home first, but after that I could take you to town. Here, get in my pocket."

And so they started. The ant wondered at the sheepherder, for he had not taken a bath in months and the smell was quite strong.

Soon the sheepherder again tripped over his own feet. This time he nearly hit a tree. On the trunk was a fat beetle sunning himself. The sheepherder's fall frightened the beetle, so he lifted himself on one elbow and apologized for scaring the beetle.

The beetle asked where he was going, and the sheepherder told him. Then the beetle asked if he might come along, for he was curious to see the inside of a rich landowner's home. And so the three continued on their journey. Once inside the sheepherder's pocket, the beetle expressed some alarm at the smell.

So the three continued until they came to a bridge. The boy

was so interested in the bridge that once again he forgot about his feet, and down he fell. This time he fell but inches from a field mouse. The field mouse immediately ran up to the boy and began to lecture him about being more careful.

Apologizing, the sheepherder offered the field mouse some of his tortilla in recompense. Once the mouse heard of the journey, he wanted to come along too. And so it happened that the ant, the beetle and the field mouse each shared the half tortilla with the sheepherder, and then climbed into his pocket for the rest of the journey.

Before too long, the travelers reached the landowner's house. The sheepherder called to the gatekeeper that he was here to try his luck. The gatekeeper opened the gate. This boy was young; it would be a shame to see him get a whipping.

When the housekeeper opened the door, she had tears in her eyes. Though whether it was from sympathy or smell, 'twas anyone's guess.

The rich landowner left his bookkeeper and met the young boy. "Are you sure you would like to try? You know you'll be whipped if you guess wrongly, boy?"

The boy nodded.

In came the daughter, dancing with the tambourine. When she finished, the rich landowner asked the boy if he knew what kind of skin the tambourine was made of—and would he *please* hurry, as the odor in the room was thickening.

The boy asked to hold the tambourine. As he moved to take it he tripped and fell to the floor. The ant was thrown from his pocket and landed on his sleeve. Getting up the boy looked closely at the tambourine. The ant crawled down the boy's sleeve and onto the tambourine. Then the ant crawled back up the sleeve to the collar of the boy's jacket and called to the sheepherder.

"Boy, this tambourine is made from a flea's skin. I know, for I've wintered and shared food with one."

The sheepherder thought it looked more like sheepskin.

Then the beetle, who was curious, crawled onto the tambourine. He was just starting to climb back up the boy's sleeve when the boy started toward the daughter, who was now crying at the smell. As he did so, down he fell again. With that, the beetle landed in his hair, edged down and hid behind the boy's ear.

The rich landowner called to the boy. "What is this tambourine made of, my boy?"

The beetle tickled the sheepherder's ear and said, "It is a flea skin. Do you hear me? Fleas are my cousins and this is a flea skin."

The sheepherder nodded his head and said, "All right, all right. It is a flea skin. I get it—it is a *flea skin!*" The sheepherder said it twice so that the beetle would stop tickling his ear.

The rich landowner stood up aghast. The daughter threw herself at her father's feet. "Please, please, Father, don't make me marry this horrible, smelly boy!"

The sheepherder put out his hand. "Just a moment," he said. "It is up to *me* to decide if I will marry you or not. Is that not right?"

"Yes, that is right. Daughter, I am a man of my word. It is up to this boy," the father said.

The beetle then whispered once again in the boy's ear. "Do not take this woman for your bride. She is spoiled and too old for you. Ask for gold instead."

The boy thought for a moment and then repeated what the beetle advised. The father and daughter were most relieved. The rich landowner asked the sheepherder how much gold he would like to have. The sheepherder pulled his pouch from his pocket, for he'd always dreamt of having his little pouch filled with gold

and said, "I would like gold to the top of this pouch as I stand here holding it."

The landowner called his bookkeeper and told him to bring the gold.

The field mouse had now awakened because there was no more falling or swaying, and he stuck his head out of the boy's pocket in order to see what was happening. When he heard the boy's last remark, he thought he ought to help. The mouse climbed down the sheepherder's sleeve and into the pouch. He then ate a good hole right through the bottom and returned to the boy's sleeve. When the bookkeeper returned to fill the pouch, the money fell at the boy's feet. But he did not move, for the mouse had now climbed onto his shoulder and was telling him to hold his hands very still and not say a word.

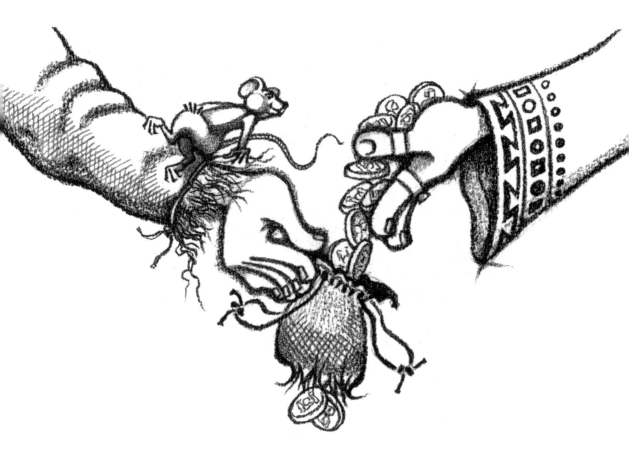

The rich landowner was as good as his word. He let the money fall through the hole until a small mountain of gold rose up to meet the top of the pouch as the patient sheepherder held it.

The landowner asked if there were any more requests, and the sheepherder, once again listening to the mouse, said, "Yes, I need a nice wagon and two good horses to help me take this money."

The landowner was only too happy to oblige.

Waving goodbye, the sheepherder then turned home. The ant, deciding this had been excitement enough, wanted to go home. The beetle was dropped off at the landowner's barn, and the mouse, well, he decided to go back with the sheepherder.

The young sheepherder married when he was sixteen. He married a girl he had known since he was little, and they lived in a nice modest little house and had many children.

The Country Mouse and the Town Mouse

UNITED KINGDOM

Once upon a time there lived a town mouse who, on a trip out to the country one day, met up with a country mouse. They spent the day together romping about in the fields and soon became fast friends. The country mouse took his new friend into the meadows and vegetable gardens, and made him sample all of the good things of the land.

Never having seen the beauties of the countryside before, the town mouse was thrilled with everything that was brought before him, though the country mouse's plain food wasn't nearly as fine as his own usual meals from town.

At the end of his visit, the town mouse wanted to thank his friend for the lovely outing, so he invited the country mouse to visit him in the town. The country mouse had never been to town before and immediately took up his friend's invitation. Together they traveled to the town and the town mouse showed his friend all the delights of town living. And when the country mouse saw the pantry at his friend's house, full of hams, cheese, oil, flour, honey, jam and stacks of other goodies, he stood speechless with surprise.

"I must say, dear friend, that I have never seen anything quite like it in all my days! Are all those wonderful looking things for eating?"

"Of course!" came the reply. "And because you are my guest, I invite you to dig in at once!"

With no further hesitation, the two friends began to feast upon the town mouse's well-stocked pantry. The country mouse tried very hard not to stuff himself. He wanted to be able to taste a little bit of everything before finding his tummy full.

"Why, you're the luckiest mouse I have ever met!" said the country mouse to his town brother. The town mouse was listening with delight to his friend's praise when suddenly, the sound of heavy footsteps interrupted their feast.

"Run for it!" whispered the town mouse to his friend. And they did. A good thing, too, because they were just in time: for within an inch of them stood the lady of the house's very large foot.

Luckily, the lady went away and the two mice were soon able to return to their former places and continue to enjoy their meal that had been so rudely interrupted.

"It's all right! Come on now!" implored the town mouse to his country friend who was a bit nervous about coming back to the pantry. "Do not worry. That lady is gone. Now for the honey! It's delicious! Have you ever tasted it?"

"Yes, once, a long time ago," the country mouse lied, trying to sound casual. But when he tasted it, he exclaimed: "Absolutely scrumptious! By the King of Mice! I have never eaten anything quite so lovely in all of my life!"

Suddenly there came the sound of footsteps, this time thumping even more heavily than before. Once again the two mice were forced to flee for their lives. The man of the house had come to fetch some bottles from the pantry, and when he saw the spilt honey, he groaned: "Why those ghastly mice again! I thought I'd gotten rid of them once and for all. I'll send the cat!"

And trembling with terror, the mice hid away.

This time it was not only the sudden visit that had given them such a fright, it was the man's awful words. The mice were so frightened, they held their breath, and tried not to make any sound at all. Time passed and when all remained quiet about them, they began to feel braver, and were able to summon enough courage to leave their hiding place and return to the pantry.

"We can come out now! There isn't anybody here!" the town mouse whispered to his friend, motioning with his paw for the other to appear.

Suddenly, the pantry door creaked, and the two luckless mice froze in fear. Out of the dim light glowed a pair of horrid yellow tiger-like eyes. A large cat was looking round the room in search of its prey. Its whiskers were tingling with the scent of nearby mice.

The country mouse and the town mouse tiptoed as silently as possible back to their hiding place. They wished their pounding hearts would stop beating, for fear the cat would hear the noise that they made.

But, as luck would have it, the cat had now discovered a juicy sausage that had slipped from the pantry to the floor. Forgetting why his master had sent him into the pantry, the cat stopped to devour the delicious-smelling sausage. After finishing its evening feast, the cat was no longer hungry. After that, it decided that it

might as well leave mouse-hunting for another day and off he padded, to have forty winks elsewhere.

Now, as soon as the country mouse realized that all immediate danger was past, he did not lose a second.

He hastily shook hands with his town mouse friend, saying: "Thanks ever so much for everything! But I really must rush off now! My heart simply cannot stand all of these shocks! I would far rather sit down in peace to a modest meal of a few acorns in the country than face a great spread of delicious food, surrounded by dangers on all sides and with my heart forever in my mouth!"

The Empress Jowka

JAPAN

There was once a good Empress who ruled over the land of Japan and its many people. She was a young, beautiful, kindly and wise lady and she was called the Empress Jowka. Empress Jowka was a peace-loving ruler who wished only the best for her people. Though she ruled all with a benevolent hand, it soon came to pass that in the northern mountains of Japan a rebellion broke out that was led by the Prince Kokai. He sent a message to the Empress by one of his footmen and his message was this:

"Empress Jowka, either you must marry me and share your throne, or I will put your kingdom to the flame and sword!"

Empress Jowka, who knew that empresses never flinch at threats, replied steadily, "Prince Kokai, you shall never receive either my kingdom or my hand. We shall fight!" And with that she sent an army to fight against the rebels in the mountains. This army was strong and well led and it easily defeated the rebels in more than one battle. But, just before the most important battle of all, something terrible and magical happened.

Prince Kokai pleaded with one of the evil gods to help him and his languishing rebel army. Soon large heavy drops began to fall upon the Empress Jowka's kingdom. In no time, the rivers grew so swollen with water that they broke their banks. There were appalling floods that quickly swept through the land and took the Imperial army by surprise, washing it away into the surrounding seas. Every man, from the general to the humblest soldier, was soon drowned in the swirling, rushing, angry water.

Once the Imperial army was vanquished, the rebellious Prince Kokai came down from the mountains and approached the capital of the Empire. Though Empress Jowka sent other armies to fight against him, each one met the same fate: they were swept away in the swirling waters that rose and fell in compliance with Prince Kokai's orders. The whole of Japan was terror-stricken. Was power to be seized by a merciless rebel magician?

Empress Jowka spent a great deal of time lost in thought and prayer over the fate of her land. One night, as she was saying her prayers, she heard a soft rustling noise coming from the corner of her room. Lifting her eyes from her clasped hands, she saw, standing in front of her, an old wizened man holding a gnarled stick and wearing a long dark tunic tied and knotted at his waist with a cord. He had long white hair that trailed down his back and a flowing white beard that was as soft as silk. The Empress jumped up in surprise, but the old man spoke calmly:

"Have no fear, Empress Jowka, I am a friend and I come in peace," he said. "I am the God of Fire. I have heard your prayers and I know how much you and your people are suffering in this battle. I know of the worry you have for your kingdom. I have come to help you. Do not worry! I shall join your armies and Prince Kokai's magic will do nothing against me."

The Empress Jowka bowed low before the old man and murmured, "Tell me, God of Fire, what must I do to help you?"

"You must gather a new army to send against the rebels. I will march at the side of your general."

The Empress nodded her head and thanked the old man. The very next morning she ordered the greatest and biggest army that had ever been mustered in Japan to appear before her. She also asked for the people of Japan to stand up for their kingdom and so a huge number of men also turned up willing to do battle. Horses and chariots completed the assembly and the newly created army set out.

Everyone, including the Imperial and rebel soldiers, knew that the battle about to be fought would be the final one. Whoever won this battle, would also rule Japan. Slowly the two opposing armies drew closer on the vast plain, and the general leading the Imperial troops murmured to his second in command:

"It is unwise to march here. Prince Kokai could easily flood this area with his evil magic!"

The God of Fire, marching at the general's side in the guise of a bold young officer replied:

"Have no fear, I am far stronger than water."

The two armies began their battle. Bravely the Imperial army defended its stance. They rushed forward, yelling and raising their swords and met the rebel soldiers head on. There were a few skirmishes, then Prince Kokai, watching the battle from high upon the mountain where he had made his camp, raised his arms and invoked the help of the elements. The earth shook and there was a fierce gust of wind that suddenly blew over the battlefield. An immense gush of water followed the wind, sweeping down the mountainside and onto the plain in fierce and swirling torrents. The Imperial soldiers screamed with terror as the rolling waves

rushed toward them, but the God of Fire, as the bold young officer, simply said:

"Keep calm! That water will not even lap at our feet."

And indeed, the huge foaming waves that seemed to gallop toward the army suddenly slowed down when they reached the God of Fire. Amazingly, the water then drew back, split in half with a tremendous roar, and was swallowed up by the earth.

"This is the end of Prince Kokai! March on!" ordered the general, and the entire army marched on toward the mountain and defeated the enemy. Prince Kokai saw that his rebellion was now over, his power depleted, and even his fortune had disappeared. But rather than surrender to the Empress Jowka, who would have forgiven him for his vengeance, he hurled himself instead, head first, against the mountain that was named Shu, and died. The blow that Prince Kokai struck against the mountain's side was so hard that a huge crack appeared. From that crack flames of furious fire appeared, followed by poisonous fumes and bubbling hot lava that quickly oozed down the mountain's side and flooded the plain below, burning and suffocating everything upon it. A far worse danger now threatened the empire of the wise Jowka!

The Empress remained calm at the news of this horrible disaster. Then she received yet another terrible piece of news. The crack in the mountain and the disaster that followed it had cracked the pillars that held up the sky, damaging the pathway along which, every day, the Sun and the Moon traveled upon their chariots carrying the light to brighten each day.

In a very short time, a dreadful dark shadow fell over all the world. The people were afraid of the darkness and they wept and despaired at the thought of no light in their lives. How could they survive in such terrifying darkness?

After much thought, the wise Empress Jowka ordered huge bonfires to be kept alight throughout the kingdom, so that the flames would give her people comfort, courage and some semblance of hope. She then sent word to all of her subjects that they should collect blue, white, orange and red stones and bring all they could of these to the palace. When this was done, the Empress herself sat down and for many days worked in the palace's cellar to grind down the stones. From the dust she made a kind of paste that resembled the texture of liquid porcelain. It was transparent and shiny.

Taking this paste she put it into a huge iron pot. Then, with a very secret and magic spell spoken softly over her special paste, she summoned a cloud to her. When the cloud arrived she climbed on top of it, carrying her pot, and asked the cloud to carry her to the exact spot where the heavenly pillar that was to hold up the sky was cracked. There, she repaired the damage using her special transparent paste. Once she had completed her task she asked the cloud to return her to the Earth. She then said to herself, "There! I have mended the pillar. The chariots of the Sun and the Moon can now take to the road again and the light will return to the land."

Alas, things did not quite happen the way that Empress Jowka had hoped! Days went by and still the light did not return. The Sun and the Moon were nowhere to be seen. And the people, who had had such high hopes in their wise and kind Empress, again began to weep and wail. They began to say, "Oh dear! We shall live the rest of our lives in the dark! We will go blind, we will die of the cold! Nothing will grow in the fields, so even if we survive in the dark and the cold, we will eventually die of hunger!"

Once again, the Empress kept her calm and pondered the dilemma. Finally, she decided to call together all the wise men of the realm and ask them to find out what it was that had happened to the land and why the Sun and the Moon did not appear as they once did.

Once the wise men had arrived, long discussions took place that lasted through the night and well into the next day. Finally a very learned philosopher went before the Empress Jowka and said:

"Your most gracious Highness, I know exactly what has happened! When the pillar of Heaven was cracked, the Sun and the Moon shut themselves away in their palaces in fright. They have never come out again. How can they possibly know now that the pillar has been repaired?"

"Yes! Yes! That is so!" chorused the other wise men.

The Empress then said, "There is only one way to tell them. We must send a messenger!"

"A messenger?" they asked, and Empress Jowka continued slowly.

"Hmm, yes. Or rather, two! One to gallop to the Sun and the other to gallop to the Moon. We must not be discourteous after all, and if we are to warn one before the other, then the second one might take offense."

All over the empire, a search was made for two horsemen brave enough to face such a long journey, and two horses strong enough to gallop into the heart of Day and Night. It wasn't easy to find suitable men but in the end, two young men approached the Empress Jowka, and she told them what had to be done . . .

The very next morning, the messengers, equipped with fine stallions and beautiful saddles, set off with their messages. They traveled a long and fearful journey that took them from cloud to cloud and from heaven to heaven. They rode through winds and storms; they brushed past comets and shooting stars. And eventually they reached their destinations and delivered the Empress's message to the Sun and the Moon.

"The pillar has been repaired," they said. "It is safe to spread your night skies and sunlight upon our earth once again."

Once again the Sun and Moon's chariots could travel safely upon the heavenly pathways. The Sun and the Moon thanked the messengers and promised to return to the earth.

The very next day, the shadows disappeared from the daylight world, and the light flooded back again, as it always had before. The two messengers knelt humbly before the Empress Jowka upon their return, but instead she made them rise to their feet, saying:

"No! Men like you shall always remain on your feet before anyone on earth, for it is only you that have looked the Sun and the Moon in the face!"

Bluebeard

FRANCE

In the fair land of France, a very long time ago, there once lived a very powerful and wealthy lord who was the owner of a great many estates, farms and even a great and splendid castle. His name was Bluebeard. Bluebeard wasn't his real name, of course, it was only his nickname. But he had received it because he had a great, long shaggy black beard that had glints of blue in it when the sun shined. He was a very handsome and charming man, but, if truth be told, there was something about him that made you feel respect, yes, but also a little bit uneasy . . .

Bluebeard would often go away to war, and when he did, he would leave his wife in charge of the castle. He had had many different wives, all of whom had been young, pretty and noble. But, as bad luck would have it, one after the other, they had soon become ill after their marriage and died, and so the noble lord seemed to be forever getting married again and again.

"Sire," someone would ask now and again, "what did your wives die of?"

"Ah, my friend," Bluebeard would reply slowly, "one died of smallpox, one of a hidden sickness, another of a high fever, another of a terrible infection . . . Ach, but I am very unlucky, and they are unlucky too! They are all buried in the castle chapel," he added.

Nobody found anything strange about all these deaths. Nor did the sweet and beautiful young girl that Bluebeard took as his latest wife think it strange either. She went to the castle, accompanied by her sister, Anna, who said to her:

"Oh, aren't you lucky to be marrying a lord like Bluebeard!"

"He really is very nice," the young bride replied, "and when you are close, his beard doesn't look quite as blue as so many folk say!" and together the two sisters giggled happily.

Poor souls! They had no idea what lay in store for them!

A month or so later, Bluebeard had the carriage brought round and he threw his many trunks into it. Then, turning to his new wife he said:

"My darling, I must leave you for a few weeks now to join the battle in the north. But keep cheerful during my time away, for I shall return. In the meantime, invite whoever you like to keep you company and look after the castle while I am gone. Here," he added, handing his bride a collection of keys on a thick iron ring, "you will need these. These are the keys to the safe, the armory and the library, and this one opens the doors to all the different rooms.

"Now, this little key here," continued Bluebeard pointing to a key on the ring that was much smaller than all of the others, "is the key that opens the little room at the very end of the ground floor corridor. Take your friends wherever you like, open any door you wish, but under no circumstances are you *ever* to open this door! Is that quite clear?" repeated Bluebeard sternly. "You must not ever open the door at the end of the ground floor corridor! Not ever! Nobody at all is allowed to enter that little room. And if you ever did go into it, I would go into such a terrible rage that really, I tell you honestly, it is far, far better that you do not!"

"Do not worry, my husband," said Bluebeard's beautiful young wife as she took the ring of keys from his hand, "I will do as you say."

After giving her a hug, Bluebeard climbed into his carriage, whipped up the horses and away he went in a great flourish of dust and noise.

The days went by. The young girl invited her friends to keep her company at the castle and showed them round all the rooms except the one at the end of the corridor.

With time she began to wonder, "Why shouldn't I see inside that little room? Why? Why is it forbidden to me?"

Well, the young bride began to think about this little room so much that the day finally came that she was so curious, she was almost bursting. She simply could not stop herself from walking down the long corridor to the door at the end of the hall, taking the ring of keys from her pocket, finding the little key that was different from all the others, and slowly opening the one door that was forbidden to her. She finally walked into the little room.

Of all ghastly horrors! Inside were the bodies of all of Bluebeard's past wives: he had strangled them all with his very own hands and hung them upon the walls!

Terror-stricken, the girl turned and ran from the room just as quickly as she could, but the bunch of keys slipped from her grasp and fell with a clatter to the stone floor. She stopped and picked them up without a glance and hurried to her own room, her heart thumping wildly in her chest. Horrors! She was living in a castle of the dead! Now she knew the truth of what had happened to all of Bluebeard's other wives!

Finally the girl summoned up enough courage to look at the ring of keys she still held in her hand. Then she noticed that one of the keys—the very key that had opened up that horrible little room—was stained with blood.

"I must wipe it clean before my husband comes back!" she said to herself. But try as she would, the bloodstain would not wash away. Though she washed and scrubbed and rinsed the key for all she was worth, it was in vain, for the key remained red.

That very evening, Bluebeard returned to his castle. Just imagine the state his poor wife was in!

Bluebeard did not ask his wife for the keys that very same evening, but he did remark to her:

"You look a little upset, my darling. Has anything nasty happened while I have been away?"

"Oh, no! No, nothing at all!" she replied, quickly.

"Are you sorry that I have come back so soon?"

"Oh, no! I am delighted!"

But that night, the bride did not sleep even a wink. The next day, Bluebeard said to her:

"Darling, give me back the keys," and his wife hurriedly did so. Bluebeard remarked: "But there is one missing, the key to the little room."

"Is there?" said the young girl, shaking, "I must have left it in my room!"

"All right then, my dear, go and get it for me and I will return it to its place."

But once Bluebeard's wife returned and put the missing key into his hand, Bluebeard turned white and in a deep hoarse voice demanded:

"Why is this key stained with blood?"

"I do not know . . ." stammered his wife.

"You know very well!" he retorted angrily. "You went into the little room, didn't you? Well, now you will go back once again, only this time for good, along with all of the other ladies in there. Now that you have disobeyed me, you must die!"

"Oh no! I pray you!" the poor wife stepped back.

"You must die!" he repeated, advancing. Just then, there was a knock at the door and Anna, the sister of Bluebeard's wife, entered the castle.

"Good morning sister and brother-in-law," she said, "you both seem rather pale this morning. Are you feeling unwell?" she asked.

"Not at all, we are both quite well," replied Bluebeard. His wife whispered in his ear:

"Please, please give me ten more minutes to live!"

Bluebeard replied: "Not more than ten!" And with that the girl ran to her sister Anna who had gone up to one of the towers and said to her quickly and quietly, "Anna, do you see our brothers coming? They promised they would come and see me today!"

But Anna replied, "No, I do not see anyone. What is wrong with you, dear sister? You look so very agitated."

"Anna, please," said the terrified girl, "look once again! Are you sure you cannot see someone coming along?"

"No," said her sister looking through the window, "only one or two peasants."

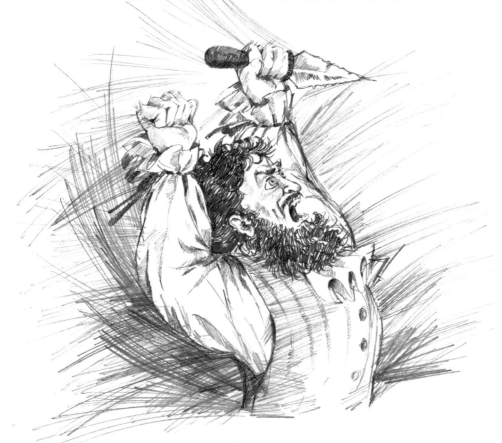

Just then the voice of Bluebeard boomed up to them:

"Wife, your time is up! Come here at once!"

"I am coming!" she called, but then said to her sister once again: "Oh Anna, aren't our brothers coming now?"

"No," replied Anna once again. Again Bluebeard shouted up.

"Come down here at once! Or I will come up!" Trembling like a leaf, his wife turned and went down the tower stairs to join her husband. Bluebeard was clutching a big carving knife and as soon as his bride entered the room he grabbed her by her hair.

Just at that very moment, Anna called down from the tower:

"Sister, I can see two horsemen coming!"

Bluebeard made a horrible face:

"Then they too will die!" he said.

His wife knelt down upon her knees and implored her husband:

"Please, please do not kill me husband. I will never tell anyone what I have seen in that room! I will never say a word!"

"That is true, wife, you will never say a word! Not for all of eternity!" and snarling, Bluebeard raised his knife above the girl's head. The poor girl screamed:

"Have pity on me!"

But he fiercely replied:

"No! You must die!"

He was about to bring the knife down on the girl's delicate throat, when two young men suddenly burst into the room: a dragoon and a musketeer. These were the brother's of Bluebeard's wife.

Taking in the horrible scene before them, they immediately drew their swords and leapt towards Bluebeard, who turned and tried to flee up some stairs, but was soon caught and killed. And that was the end of the sad story.

Bluebeard's poor wives were given a Christian burial, the castle was completely rebuilt and the young widow, some time later, married a good and honest young man, who helped her to forget her terrible adventure. And that young lady also completely lost all her sense of curiosity . . .

The Poplar and the Stream

RUSSIA

There once was a woodcutter who lived by himself in the middle of a huge forest in the north end of Russia. This woodcutter was called Ivan and he was a very sturdy young man. With his bare hands he built himself a handsome and stout log cabin and when it was finished, he thought to himself that since he was young, had a good job and a good house, all that he needed was a good wife and his life would be complete. His dream was to find a beautiful young maiden who was tall, slender and fair, with blue eyes and a creamy skin.

On Sundays, Ivan would roam to distant villages and search for the girl of his dreams. But the only girls he ever saw were dull and not nearly pretty enough for him.

As it so happened, the path he would take to work each day passed close to a pretty little house with green shutters. Often, the corner of a curtain would be raised as Ivan stepped by and a sweet-faced girl would watch the woodcutter as he walked to his work. Little did Ivan know, but he had unwittingly lit the flames of love

in a young maiden's heart. This young girl was called Natasha; she was very shy, but her love for the woodcutter was so great that, one day, she plucked up enough courage to stop him on the path.

"I have picked this basket of strawberries myself," she said to the handsome young woodcutter, holding the straw basket before her. "Please eat them and think of me!" she said sweetly.

"Well, she is not exactly ugly," said Ivan to himself as he stared woodenly at Natasha, who stood blushing to the very roots of her hair.

"I do not like strawberries," Ivan replied bluntly. "But thanks all the same!" and with a wave and nary a backward glance, Ivan continued his way down the path.

Tears of sadness and humiliation sprang to Natasha's eyes as she watched her love stride away. A few days later, the girl stopped Ivan once again. This time she held out a woolen jacket saying:

"The air will be chilly tonight when you go home. This will keep you warm. I have made it myself with only the very best wool. Please take it and think of me."

But Ivan coldly replied: "What makes you think that a strong man like me would be afraid of a little cold?" And away he marched without another glance.

And this time, at Ivan's bitter refusal, two tears slowly rolled down Natasha's rosy cheeks and she turned and fled, sobbing, back into the house.

Crushed as Natasha was, her heart was steadfast and again the very next day she watched for the woodcutter along the path. This time, she held out a beautiful handblown bottle and said:

"You cannot refuse a liqueur that I distilled from all the fruits of the forest! It will . . . ." But Ivan quickly broke in saying: "I do not like liqueurs of any kind," and once again marched straight on into the forest. However, this time he realized he had been very rude, so he soon turned round to apologize, but Natasha had gone.

As he walked, he said to himself: "She has gentle eyes, and she must be very kindhearted to offer me so many gifts! Perhaps I should accept at least one of her gifts, but . . . ." The picture of his dream girl slipped into his mind. "I am so unhappy!" he sighed.

At that very moment, a beautiful lady suddenly appeared in front of Ivan, floating on a golden cloud. "Will you sing a song for me? I am Rosalka, one of the woodland fairies!" Ivan stood thunderstruck.

"I would sing for you for the rest of my life!" he exclaimed, "If only I could . . . ." and he stretched out his hand to touch the fairy, but she floated out of reach amongst the branches.

"Sing then! Sing! Only the sound of your voice will ever send me to sleep!" she said above him.

So Ivan happily sang all of the old lullabies and love songs that he knew, while the drowsy fairy continued to urge him on: "Sing! Sing!"

Cold and weary, his voice becoming more and more hoarse, the woodcutter sang through the evening, trying in vain to help the fairy to fall asleep. But when night fell, Rosalka was still demanding: "If you love me, sing on! Sing!"

And so, Ivan the woodcutter sang on through the night, in a feeble voice, and he kept thinking to himself: "I wish I had a jacket to keep me warm!"

Suddenly he remembered Natasha.

"What a fool I am!" he thundered aloud. "I should have chosen her as my bride, and not this woman who asks and gives nothing in return!"

Ivan felt that only the gentle-faced Natasha could fill his empty heart. He fled into the darkness, but he heard a cruel voice call: "You will never see her again! All the tears she has shed for her great love have turned her into a stream! You will never see her again!"

It was dawn when Ivan finally arrived at the pretty little cottage in the wood and knocked at Natasha's door. But alas, no one answered. And though the woodcutter continued to knock and pound upon the door, nothing stirred from within. And finally the woodcutter saw, with fear, that close by the cottage flowed a tiny sparkling stream that he had never noticed before. Weeping sorrowfully, he walked over to it and plunged his face into the water.

"Oh, Natasha, my dearest love, how could I have been so blind? But I love you now and forever!" he exclaimed and lifting his gaze to the sky, he silently said a prayer: "Let me stay beside her forever!"

And suddenly Ivan was turned into a young poplar tree on the bank of the sparkling river. And as the stream lapped and bathed at the poplar's roots, Natasha had, at last, her beloved Ivan by her side forever more.

The Story of Thumbelina

GERMANY

Once upon a time there lived a lonely old woman in a pretty little house in a wood by a pasture. This woman had no children of her own and passed each day doing her chores and cleaning her pretty little house. Every day she would dream of having a little girl who she could take care of and love, but as time went by, her dream never came true.

Finally, tired of being alone and kept company only by her dreams, she decided to go and visit a witch that she knew lived deep within the forest. The witch gave her a single magic grain of barley and told her to take it home and carefully plant it in a pot. The woman took the magic grain and wrapped it up in a lace handkerchief and carried it all the way home. Then, taking her most beautiful flowerpot from a shelf, she planted the magic barley grain in the flowerpot. She used only the richest and darkest earth and carefully watered the grain when she was finished. Then she took the beautiful flowerpot and placed it carefully on her windowsill, right beside her bed.

The very next day, when the woman woke with the sun, as she did each day, she reached up to look into the flowerpot and see what had become of the magic grain. Sure enough, in the rich, dark earth, there now was a lovely flower reaching up toward the morning sun. The flower looked rather like a tulip. The woman was so touched by the flower's fragile beauty, she leaned over to softly kiss its half-shut petals. And as though by magic, the flower suddenly opened in full blossom.

Inside sat a tiny girl, perfect in every way, but no bigger than a thumb. The woman decided to call her Thumbelina. For a bed Thumbelina had a walnut shell, violet petals for her mattress and a rose petal for her blanket. In the daytime, she would play in a tulip petal boat, and float upon a plate of water. Using two horse-hairs as oars, Thumbelina would sail around her little lake each day and sing and sing in a gentle sweet voice as the lady worked about her house.

Then one night, as Thumbelina lay fast asleep in her little walnut shell, a large frog hopped through a hole in the window pane. As the ugly green frog gazed down at the sleeping Thumbelina, she said to herself: "How pretty she is! She would make the perfect bride for my own dear son!"

So the frog picked up little Thumbelina, walnut shell and all, and hopped away into the garden. Nobody saw the frog and Thumbelina disappear, and the woman never knew what happened to her precious little girl.

Back at the pond, the frog's fat ugly son, who always did as his mother told him, was very pleased with her choice of bride. But mother frog was afraid that her pretty little prisoner might run away. So she carried Thumbelina out to a water lily leaf in the middle of the pond.

"She can never escape us now," said the frog to her son, "And

now we have plenty of time to prepare a new home for you and your bride."

Thumbelina was left all alone and stranded upon the lily pad. She felt terribly desperate, but she knew that she would never be able to escape the fate that awaited her with the two horrid fat frogs. So, as she waited for her wedding day to come, she sat upon the lily pad and cried many tears that simply fell into the pond, one after the other.

It just so happened that two minnows who had been enjoying the shade below the water lily leaf had overheard the two frogs talking, and also the little girl's bitter sobs. Feeling sorry for the helpless girl, they decided that they must do something about her dreadful situation. They decided to nibble away at the stem upon the lily pad where Thumbelina sat, until it broke and drifted away in the weak current. A butterfly that was dancing in the sunlight ahead saw Thumbelina drift away on the current and, charmed by the little girl's beauty and sad little face, suddenly had an idea: "Throw me the end of your belt! I will help you to move a little faster!" she called to the little girl.

Thumbelina gratefully did so, and the leaf soon floated away from the horrible frog pond.

But other dangers lay ahead. A large beetle that was sitting by the edge of a pond saw Thumbelina float by on her little lily pad nest and suddenly snatched her from the leaf with its four strong feet and took her away to his home at the top of a leafy tree.

"Isn't she pretty?" he said to his friends. But the other beetles pointed out that she was far too different looking to be pretty to them. So the beetle took her down the tree once again and set her free.

It was summer time now and Thumbelina wandered amongst the flowers and through the long grass all by herself. She ate pollen from the flowers for her meals and drank the glistening dew that clung to the flower's petals with each fresh morning. Then the rainy season came, bringing with it nasty weather. The poor child soon found it hard to find food and shelter. When winter set in, she suffered from the cold and felt terrible pangs of hunger.

One day, as Thumbelina roamed helplessly over the bare meadows, she met a large spider who promised to help her. He took her to a hollow tree and guarded the door with a stout web. Then he brought her some dried chestnuts and called his friends to come and admire her beauty. But just like the beetles, all the other spiders persuaded Thumbelina's rescuer to let her go. She did not look like they did and they did not like her strange looks.

Quite desperate now and weeping profusely, certain that nobody wanted her because she was ugly, Thumbelina left the spider's house.

As she wandered once again through the meadows, shivering with the cold, she suddenly came across a solid little cottage, made of twigs and dead leaves. Hopefully, she knocked on the door. It was opened by a field mouse.

"What are you doing outside in this weather?" he asked. "Come in and warm yourself by the fire."

Comfortable and cozy, the field mouse's home was stocked with plenty of food for the long winter ahead. For her keep, the field mouse and Thumbelina decided that she would do the housework and keep the mouse entertained with stories. One day, the field mouse said a friend would be coming to visit them.

"He is a very rich mole, and has a lovely house not too far from here. He wears a splendid black fur coat, but he is dreadfully shortsighted. He is lonely and needs company and he would like to marry you!"

Thumbelina did not relish the idea of being married to a mole. However, when the mole came, she sang sweetly to him and he soon fell head over heels in love with her. The mole invited Thumbelina and the field mouse to his house, but when they went to visit him, to their surprise and horror, they came upon a swallow in the tunnel. It looked dead. Mole nudged it with his foot, saying: "That will teach her! She should have come underground instead of darting about the sky all summer!"

Thumbelina was so shocked by the cruel words that mole had uttered that later, she crept back unseen to help the swallow in the tunnel.

And each and every day, the little girl went to tenderly nurse the swallow and give it food.

In the meantime, the swallow told Thumbelina its tale. Impaled by a thorn, it had been unable to follow its companions to a warmer climate and instead it had fallen into this tunnel.

"It's kind of you to nurse me," it told Thumbelina.

But, the following spring, once the swallow had recovered from its injuries, it flew away, after offering to take the little girl with it. All summer, Thumbelina did her best to avoid marrying the mole. The little girl thought fearfully of how she would have to live underground forever. On the eve of her wedding, she asked to spend the day in the open air. As she gently fingered a flower, she heard a familiar song: "Winter is on its way and I will be off to warmer lands. Come with me!"

It was the swallow who had spotted the little girl from above and flown down to entice her once again to come with him. This time Thumbelina did not hesitate and quickly jumped onto the swallow's back and clung to her friend's neck. The bird soared into the sky. They flew over plains and hills till they reached a country of flowers.

The swallow gently laid Thumbelina in a blossom. There she met a tiny, white-winged fairy, the King of the Flower Fairies.

Instantly, upon seeing the beautiful and tiny little girl, he asked her to marry him. Thumbelina eagerly said "yes," and sprouting tiny white wings, she became the Flower Queen!

Dopey Dennis

UNITED KINGDOM

There was once a little boy called Dennis who lived in a small town in England. Everyone called him Dopey rather than Dennis, because, well, as you read on you will see why. Dennis lived alone with his mother in a nice little house with a courtyard, vegetable plot, cellar and a henrun.

One day, Dennis' mother had to go out and do some shopping. She said to her boy, "I will be away for an hour or two, my son. Now, the broody hen is sitting on her eggs. Make sure that nobody goes near her. Keep the house tidy and do not touch the jar in the cupboard, it is full of poison. Do you understand me?"

"Don't worry, Mum," the little boy said. And once his mother had gone to run her errands, he went into the yard and sat on an overturned wooden crate to keep guard over the broody hen. However, the hen soon grew tired of sitting and decided to get up to stretch her legs for a little before going back to her eggs. When Dennis saw the hen get up, he immediately picked up a stick and waving it at the hen, yelled:

"You nasty creature, get right back on those eggs!"

But the broody hen was annoyed with the loud little boy and only said:

"Cluck!" in reply.

So Dennis hit her with his stick. He didn't really mean to do her any harm, but the blow fell on the middle of her neck and the poor hen suddenly dropped down dead.

"Oh!" gasped the young lad. "Now who is going to sit on the eggs?" and he stood in the yard and scratched his head and pondered his dilemma. "Well, I had better do something about that!" he said finally, and so he walked over to the hen's nest and sat down upon the eggs . . . and broke the lot!

Getting up with the seat of his trousers now sticky with egg yolk, Dennis said to himself, "Oh dear. Mum will give me such a scolding when she finds out about this. But to keep her happy, I will give her a surprise. I'll make a fine lunch." And he picked up the dead hen, plucked its feathers and put it on the spit to roast.

"A roast calls for a good wine!" he said to himself. He took a jug and went down to the cellar where he started to draw sparkling red wine from a barrel.

"Mum will be pleased with me," he said to himself. At that moment, there was a dreadful noise in the kitchen. Dennis said to himself, "Who can that be? I must go and see." And up the stairs of the cellar he went, forgetting to turn off the tap on the wine barrel.

Up he ran to the kitchen and saw that it was the cat with the roast hen in its jaws and the spit overturned.

"Hey, you little thief!" shouted the lad. "Put my hen down!"

He picked up a rolling pin and started to chase the cat around the room. The cat, terrified as it was, firmly held on to the roast chicken as it dashed from room to room. The pair of them knocked against the cupboards, overturned tables, sideboards and stools, smashed vases, pots, plates and glasses. The devastation ended when the cat finally dropped the hen, leapt out of a window and vanished from sight. Dennis picked up his roast, laid it on the table and said:

"Now, I will go and fetch the wine."

He went back down the stairs of the cellar and stopped in amazement at the bottom of the stairs. The cellar was flooded with the wine that had poured out of the barrel when Dennis had disappeared to investigate the noise upstairs, forgetting to turn off the tap.

"Good gracious!" gasped Dennis. "What am I to do now?" He did not dare go any further into the cellar, for before him stretched a lake of red wine.

"I will have to mop it all up," muttered Dennis to himself, "but how, and with what? I suppose I could go into the yard and gather some sacks of sand, bring them into the cellar and scatter the sand over the floor . . . . But that seems like an awful lot of hard work to do. I had better think of something else."

Seated on the bottom step of the cellar, his elbows firmly upon his knees, and holding his head in his hands, the lad tried to think of a good way to clean up the cellar. It really was an alarming situation: there were nearly six inches of wine all over the floor and in it floated corks, bottles and bits of wood.

"I've got it!" Dennis suddenly exclaimed.

He picked up one of the bags lying on a table, opened it, and started to scatter all the flour it contained upon the floor.

"Splendid! This flour will absorb the wine and I can then walk about the cellar without wetting my feet," he cried.

In no time at all, he had spread not one, but five bags of good, expensive flour about upon the floor. In the end, the floor was covered with a wine-colored, soft, sticky paste, and as he walked on it, it stuck to the bottom of his shoes. Dennis went to get the wine jug he had filled and carried it in great delight back upstairs to the table, leaving red footprints everywhere he went.

"Mum is going to be really pleased," he said.

Nevertheless, when he thought of all the mess he had made, he began to fear a scolding and maybe punishment, too.

"Never mind," he said, "I will drink the poison and die, and that way Mum will not be able to punish me."

So he went to the cupboard and picked up the jar. He thought the poison would be a black liquid, but the jar contained a red cream. He picked up a spoon and said, "I will eat it then instead of drinking it."

Just as he was about to take his first spoonful, he realized how silly he was. Nobody should ever eat poison, not even when your name is Dopey Dennis. Instead, he decided to hide from his mother so that she would not be able to punish him.

A quarter of an hour later, his mother returned from her errands. When she saw the overturned furniture, the broken plates and dishes and the red footprints everywhere, she got quite a fright and cried out, "Dennis! What has happened? Where are you? Answer me!"

There was no reply, but she suddenly noticed a pair of legs sticking out of the oven.

"Well, I'm not surprised to see that you are hiding from me, Dennis, after causing all of this mess," she said. "While I am clearing up after you, you can take this roll of cloth to the market and try and sell it for a good price." And when Dennis had appeared from the oven and dusted the ash from his hair and his clothes, she handed the boy a roll of cloth as she spoke.

"Oh, yes Mum, I will," said Dennis. "Leave it to me."

When he got to the market, Dennis began to shout, "Cloth! Who will buy this lovely cloth?"

Several women came over and asked him, "What kind of cloth is it? Is it soft? Is it hard-wearing? Is it dear? How long is it? How much does it cost?"

Dennis exclaimed: "My goodness, but all of you talk too much, and I do not sell things to chatterboxes," and off he went, carrying the cloth with him.

He passed by a statue that stood on the corner of the road and mistook it for a fine gentleman, so he asked it, "Sir, would you like to buy this fine cloth, yes or no?" When the statue did not reply to Dennis, being a statue and not capable of speaking, Dennis then said, "If you don't say anything, that means you do want to buy this cloth. Look here! Do you like it? Yes? Good! Then take it," and he left the cloth beside the statue and went on home.

"Mum! Mum!" he cried. "I have sold the cloth to a very well-dressed gentleman!"

The woman asked: "Well, that's good news my boy. How much did he give you for it?"

Dennis muttered, "Oh! I forgot to ask him for the money! Don't worry mum, I'll go and ask him for it now."

He ran back to the statue but the cloth had disappeared. Clearly someone had taken it away.

Said Dennis to the statue, "I see you have taken the cloth home already. Fine, now you must give me the money!"

Of course, the statue did not reply.

Dennis repeated his request, then losing his temper, he picked up a nearby stick and began to beat the statue about the head. Suddenly the head broke off and rolled to the ground. Out of the head poured a handful of gold coins, hidden there by goodness knows who! Dennis picked up the coins, put the head back in position on top of the statue and went on home.

"Look!" he called once he'd stepped in the door. And his mother stared in astonishment at the small fortune he held before her.

"Who gave you such a good price?" his mother asked him. The lad replied: "A very dignified-looking gentleman. He didn't speak, and do you know where he kept his money? In his head!"

At this, Dennis's mother exclaimed: "Dennis, listen! You killed the broody hen, broke the eggs, flooded the cellar with wine, wasted five bags of flour, smashed plates, bottles, vases and glasses; you nearly ate the cream, if you think you're going to pull my leg as well you're badly mistaken! Now get out of here, you naughty boy!"

And grabbing the broom, she chased him out of the house.

"I don't want to see you again until tonight! Off you go into the vegetable plot."

But, as the boy was sitting on the doorstep and did not budge for anything his mother might say, his exasperated mother picked up the first thing that came within her grasp and hurled it at Dennis's head. It was a big basket of dried figs and sultanas.

Dennis shouted then: "Mum! Mum! Quick! Bring a bag! It's raining dry figs and sultanas!"

At this, Dennis's mother slumped into a chair and said sorrowfully: "What can I do with a boy like him?"

Now, since Dennis went about telling all the folk in the village that he had a lot of gold coins, the magistrates finally sent for him.

"Where did you find those coins?" they asked him.

Dennis replied: "A gentleman gave me them in payment for a roll of cloth."

"What gentleman was this?" said the magistrates severely.

"The gentleman that is always standing at the corner of Plane Tree Street and Jasmine Road," replied the boy.

"But that is a statue!" gasped the magistrates. Dennis said: "He did not say what his name was, but maybe it is Mr. Statue. He kept his money in his head."

The magistrates gaped at each other in utter astonishment.

Then the chief magistrate asked: "Tell us, Dennis, on what day did you do this piece of business?"

"It was the day it rained dry figs and sultanas!" the boy replied.

Again the magistrates exchanged looks, and now certain that Dennis really was dopey, they said: "You can go home, lad, you're free to go!"

And so Dennis went home and lived there happily with his mother. A bit dopey, yes, but he never did any person any harm, and that is all that counts.

Sayed's Adventures

INDIA

A very long time ago, in the mysterious and exotic land of the East, there once lived a man called Benezar who married a woman called Zemira. They were in love with each other and agreed on all things, except one. Zemira believed in magic, omens, premonitions and fairies. Benezar only believed in what he could see plainly before his eyes and not a whit else. However, this one disagreement did not mar the couple's happiness at all, and this reached its height, when, one day, in the midst of a thunderstorm, Zemira gave birth to a handsome baby boy.

When Benezar, who had anxiously awaited the newborn's arrival, was allowed into the delivery room to see the baby, he noticed a tiny whistle hanging from a thin silver thread round its neck.

"What is this?" he asked, lifting the delicate whistle between his fingertips.

"It is a gift a fairy has made to our son," replied Zemira. "It is a magic gift. Take it," she went on, removing the whistle from the child's neck, "and give it to our son when he reaches the age of twenty, and not a day sooner."

"All right, dear wife. I will humor your strange fancies. But listen, by what name shall we call the child?" asked Benezar fondly.

"Sayed," replied Zemira.

The years went by and Sayed grew to be healthy, strong and brave. Sadly, his mother did not live to see him enter adulthood and died of a fever when he was only six. When the boy was eighteen years old, he decided to go on a pilgrimage to the holy city of Mecca. He told his father of his decision.

"Yes, I am pleased to hear that you are going," said his father. "In fact, Sayed, take this as a lucky charm," and he pulled the fairy's gift, the whistle on its delicate silver chain, from a box in the drawer of a cabinet and gave it to him.

"What is it?" Sayed asked.

"It is a whistle. Your dear mother, alas now dead, thought highly of it. Carry it with you always and think of her."

"I will Father," said the young man, and carefully put the whistle round his neck.

Not long after, the many travelers who intended to travel the pilgrimage turned out. There were a hundred camels, many merchants and a host of guards, who also set out on the journey. Young Sayed was splendidly equipped and armed with a sword, spear, bow and arrows.

It was a long, long way to the holy city of Mecca. The pilgrims traveled over plains, mountains and deserts. It was on a long stretch of desert that they were suddenly attacked by a large band of robbers. They were caught unaware and when some of the pilgrims attempted to flee, Sayed shouted: "Flee? Where do you think you can flee to in the desert? Come on. Let us at least die fighting!" and he hurled himself against the attackers. At the height of the fighting, Sayed was attacked by a young robber, richly dressed and riding a white horse. The young man bravely faced his attacker and killed him with his sword. A soldier nearby shouted out, "What have you done? You have killed Almansor. This is the end, let us run!"

Men ran and scattered in all directions. Now practically alone, Sayed remembered the whistle round his neck. If it really was magic, he thought, it might be able to help him. He put the whistle to his lips and blew hard, but nothing happened. Not so much as a whisper of sound was to be heard.

In the meantime, the others had fled. Sayed was taken prisoner, bound and led before Sheik Selim, a very powerful man, and the leader of several of the desert tribes and also, unfortunately for Sayed, the father of Almansor, the very man Sayed had killed. Selim, however, was not an unjust man. When he discovered that Sayed had taken Almansor's life in a fair fight, he refused to allow a hair of his head to be harmed. Indeed, he set him free and entrusted the young man to some travelers about to leave for far-off Mecca, the holy city.

Sayed thus found himself once more upon the route of his original travels. However, one night, friends of the dead Almansor captured him.

"Your master told you not to kill me," cried the young man as he struggled against his attackers.

"We are not going to kill you. All we are going to do is tie you up and leave you here in the desert. Thirst and the sun, or the vultures or the jackals will do what we cannot. They, not us, will kill you!" And laughing cruelly, they bound Sayed up hand and foot and they rode away.

Two whole days went by. Sayed was on the point of death, baked as he was by the sun. With no water to quench his thirst and no shade to cover his brow, he feared his end was near. Finally, some travelers belonging to Kalum the merchant swept close by and heard his feeble cries. They came to his aid and saved his life.

As he came back to his senses with the first sips of water, Sayed spoke: "May Allah reward you, sir, for saving my life. What is your name?"

"My name is Kalum," said the man, "but it will not be Allah who will reward me. You are going to do that yourself. If I had not come along, you would have been dead by now. And you are going to work for me until you have repaid that debt. What is your name?"

"Sayed," he answered.

"Well, Sayed, get up and come with me." The young man went along with Kalum and as they traveled together he discovered that he was a rich merchant from Baghdad, so that was the city in ·which Sayed went to live.

At that time, Baghdad was ruled by the famous Caliph, Harun-el-Rascid, a wise, valiant ruler who was loved by all. Kalum owned a big bazaar in the city and it was there that Sayed was put to work doing all of the humble jobs.

One day, a veiled woman came to the bazaar. Sayed was amazed when she said to him, "You are Sayed, are you not?"

"Yes," he replied in astonishment. "How did you know my name?"

"Tell me," the woman replied, ignoring his question, "have you still got the whistle round your neck?"

"Why, yes of course!" exclaimed the young man in astonishment. "You must be the fairy who gave it to my mother. But what is this whistle for? I have tried blowing upon it, but . . ."

The woman interrupted him.

"It will be of no use to you until you have reached the age of twenty. Then it will save your life. Now tell me, what can I do for you?"

"Help me to get home," Sayed replied. "I need lots of money for that, which I do not have."

"But you are young, brave and strong. You can earn it," said the woman, and she explained that every week, tournaments were held in the city, and Harun-el-Rascid, the Caliph, would always make a point of watching them. The winners received rich prizes. The veiled woman had weapons, armor and horses and she lent these to Sayed saying that he should use them to the best of his ability in the competitions. So he took part in the tournaments and because he was young and strong he always beat the others, and he received a great many prizes, as well as the Caliph's admiration. Sayed, however, would never reveal his name; he would only mention that he was a horseman from distant Cairo.

Now it so happens that the Caliph, Harun-el-Rascid, liked to wander through the city at night, disguised as a beggar or merchant, to hear what folk had to say about him. The Caliph was not interested in spying on his people, only to try and put right any mistakes he might have made through his rule. From time to time, he was accompanied on these nightly rides by his Chief Minister.

Well, one night, as Sayed was going home to Kalum's bazaar, he heard shouts and the sounds of a struggle nearby. Four men had attacked two others in a dark corner. The brave young man immediately came to the rescue of the two who had been set upon in the dark by killing two of the attackers and chasing the other two away. When it was all over, the two victims thanked Sayed for his assistance and for saving their lives and asked him, "Brave youth, what is your name so that we may know who has saved us?"

"My name is Sayed," came the reply, "and I am the shop assistant to the merchant Kalum."

"Hmm," said one of the two men, "you seem to me to be more of a gentleman than a shop assistant. However, take this ring as a reward for what you have done for me."

Then the other man spoke. "And take also this bag of coins. You have saved my life and you deserve it. Good-bye!"

And away they went.

Sayed stood there with the ring and the bag of coins in his hand. With these he could now find a ship and go home.

The very next day he said to Kalum, "I am leaving. I won't be working for you any longer."

"And where are you going?" asked Kalum.

"Home!" answered Sayed.

"Home? But that is a costly journey, and with the wages I pay you . . . ."

Sayed only smiled and said, "It is true that your pay certainly would not take me far, but you see," and he held out the bag of gold, "this money will. Farewell!"

However, wicked Kalum was not to be so easily defeated. He told the police that Sayed had stolen a bag of gold. The young man was immediately arrested. The chief of police asked him, "Who gave you this money?"

"A man I had never seen before," was the honest reply.

Sayed was judged a thief and sentenced to deportation to Thirsty Island, the home of the worst kind of criminals.

On the ship the young man thought to himself, "Well, I left home two years ago, proud, rich and happy. Here I am today, twenty years old, in the midst of these convicts, condemned to live and die an innocent man in prison!"

During the night there was a terrible storm. Driven by the wind, the ship was flung about by the waves until it crashed onto some hidden rocks.

Only one man survived the disaster. It was Sayed. At the mercy of the waters, he groped for something to hold on to, but nothing came within his grasp, until suddenly he felt his fingers touch the whistle the fairy had given him. Desperately, he blew into it with his very last ounce of strength and wind. Suddenly, a dolphin surfaced beside him, shaking its head as though to tell him to get upon its back. Sayed clambered onto the dolphin's back and there found safety in the turbulent waters. As he sailed through the waters on the dolphin's back he remembered what the fairy at the bazaar had told him. Once he reached twenty years, the whistle round his neck would save his life! The dolphin carried the young man within sight of land.

"Thanks, friend!" called Sayed as he slid down from the kind creature's back and swam ashore. What a surprise awaited him! Sayed had swam ashore to a military camp, complete with soldiers and war machines. Sayed was immediately taken prisoner and brought before none other than Harun-el-Rascid himself. The soldiers who had seized him said, "Sire, this man must be one of the convicts that survived the shipwreck."

"Is that so?" Harun-el-Rascid demanded gravely.

"Yes," replied Sayed honestly, "I did survive the shipwreck. But I am not a convict."

And he explained to Harun-el-Rascid how he had been reported to the police because of the bag of gold. "It was given to me," he went on, "by one of two men I saved one night from being attacked by four robbers." Harun-el Rascid looked at the man sitting beside him and then said, "Did the two men give you anything else?"

"Yes, they did in fact. I was also given this ring," Sayed replied, showing the Caliph the ring which he kept round his neck with the whistle. Harun rose to his feet and exclaimed: "Young man, the two men you helped were my Chief Minister and myself! Go free, but first tell me your name."

"Sayed, Sire."

"Sayed, you say?" echoed the Chief Minister. "There is a man here in the camp called Benezar, who is searching for his son, Sayed."

"But that must be my father!" cried the young man.

And it was his father. And when they were brought together after such a long absence, they hugged each other in delight.

Since justice must be done in the world, evil Kalum was arrested and imprisoned as he deserved to be and Sayed lived a long and happy life with his father by his side and his whistle forever on its chain around his neck.

The Ruby Prince

PERSIA

There once lived a beggar in far away Persia who, luckily for him, had a sudden stroke of luck. After what had been a sudden flood, the fast-flowing river near the capital city shrank back into its old bed, leaving a trail of mud and slime behind it on the banks of the town's river. In the dirt, the beggar, who had been walking along slowly, suddenly caught sight of a sparkling red stone. He picked it up, and clutching it to him, hurried off to visit one of his friends who worked in the royal kitchens at the court.

"How many dinners would you give me for this lovely shining stone?" he asked the man hopefully.

"But this is a ruby!" exclaimed the cook. "You must take it to the Shah at once!"

So the very next day, the beggar took the stone to the Shah, who asked him: "Where did you find this?"

"Lying in the mud on the bank of the river, Sire!" he said.

"Hmm!" mused the Shah. "Now why would the great river leave such a treasure to someone like you? I will give you a bag of gold for the stone. Will that do?"

The beggar could scarcely believe his ears.

"Sire, this is the most wonderful day of my life," he stammered. "My most humble thanks!" he said, bowing low toward the ground.

The Shah's courtiers then took the ruby from the beggar, and as the Shah had instructed, gave the man a bag of gold in return. The beggar gratefully took the bag of gold and left the palace happier than he could ever remember being in his life.

Before the Shah locked the big stone in his treasure box, he called to Fatima, his daughter, and said: "This is the biggest ruby that I have ever seen. I shall give it to you for your eighteenth birthday!"

Fatima admired the sparkling red gem in her hand and happily threw her arms round her father's neck.

"It is marvelous, Father! Thank you ever so much. I know it will bring me good luck!"

Some months later, on the day of Fatima's eighteenth birthday, the Shah went to fetch the ruby from his treasure box and bring it to his daughter as he had promised. But when he lifted the lid of the

box, he leapt back in surprise, for out stepped a handsome young man, who smilingly said, "The ruby you want no longer exists! I have taken its place. I am the Ruby Prince. Please do not ask me how this miracle took place. It is a secret that I can never reveal!"

Once the Shah had gotten over his shock, he went into a towering rage.

"I lose a precious gem, find a prince, and I am not even allowed to ask the reason why?" he roared.

"I am sorry, Sire," replied the prince, "but nothing and nobody will ever make me tell how it is that I have gotten here."

Furious at these words, the Shah instantly decided to punish the young man for his impertinence.

"Since you have taken the place of my ruby," he thundered, "you are now to be my servant, I presume."

"Of course, Sire," replied the young man confidently.

"Good!" exclaimed the Shah. "Then take my gold sword. I will reward you with the hand of my daughter, Fatima, if you succeed in killing the dragon of Death Valley that is stopping the caravans from passing through the forest."

As it happens, many a brave young man had already lost his life trying to kill the terrible dragon that the Shah spoke of, and it was for this reason that the Shah had announced this deed. He was quite certain the Ruby Prince would never be able to slay the fearsome dragon and he would share the same fate of the other brave young men.

However, the Ruby Prince gladly accepted his task, and armed with the Shah's sword, he set off for Death Valley. He traveled for many days and nights before he reached the edge of the thick dark forest that was Death Valley. He then called out loudly for the dragon to reveal itself. But the only reply to his call was the echo of his own voice.

Leaning against a tree trunk, the Ruby Prince was about to drop off to sleep when the sound of snapping branches brought him quickly to his feet. A frightful hissing sound grew steadily louder and louder and suddenly the earth trembled beneath the prince's feet and the terrible dragon came toward him.

The huge horrible beast reared back on two gigantic and scaly green legs and opened up its huge jaws, revealing a forked tongue and magnificently sharp teeth. Unlike all the other brave warriors who had gone before him to slay this terrible beast, the prince steadfastly stood his ground in the face of such terrifyingly evil power and strength. Suddenly, before the dragon had even a moment to consider, he took a quick step forward and struck first one heavy blow at the dragon's throat with the golden sword, then another, till at last the monster lay dead at his feet.

When he finally returned to the palace carrying the dragon's head upon his horse, the Ruby Prince was hailed as a hero. He had defeated the horrible dragon that had killed so many before him. And so, true to his promise, the Shah held a grand wedding where Fatima and the Ruby Prince were married and lived together a happy life.

However, as time passed, Fatima gradually became more and more curious about her husband's mysterious past.

"I know nothing about you," she would complain. "At least tell me who you really are and where you once lived!"

But every time the Ruby Prince heard his wife utter such remarks, he went white in the face and replied, "My wife, please do not ask me such questions. You know that I cannot tell you. You must not ask again, or you will run the risk of losing me forever!"

But Fatima was tormented by the mystery of her husband and her desire to resolve it.

One day, as they sat together by the river that flowed through the Shah's gardens, Fatima pleaded with him once again to reveal his secret to her.

White-faced, the young man replied, "But Fatima, my darling, I cannot!"

But Fatima only pleaded more: "Oh, please! Please tell me! I cannot live without knowing the truth!" she cried.

"You know, my sweet, that I cannot . . ."

The Ruby Prince hesitated, gazing at his dearly loved wife's beautiful face and gently stroked her silken hair. Then he made his decision.

"I do not wish to see you suffer like this any further. If you really must know, then I will tell you that I am . . ."

At the very moment that the Ruby Prince was about to reveal his secret, a huge wave suddenly leapt out from the river and swept him back into it, dragging him under the water.

The horrified princess rushed vainly along the bank, crying loudly for her husband. But he had vanished from sight and sound completely. Fatima called to the guards but alas, the prince was not to be found.

The Shah himself ran to comfort his grieving daughter. But the princess became very depressed and was not to be consoled. For she knew that she and she alone was responsible for this horrible tragedy. Had it not been for her foolish and insistent questioning, her husband would still be with her today.

One day, her favorite handmaiden hurried up to her.

"Your Highness!" she exclaimed. "I saw the most amazing thing last night as I walked along the river. A host of tiny lights appeared on the river from nowhere, and then a thousand little genies suddenly draped the river bank with flowers. Such a handsome young man then began to dance in honor of an old man who seemed to be a king. And beside the king there stood a young man with a ruby upon his forehead. I thought he was . . . ."

Fatima's heart leapt when she heard her handmaiden's story: could the young man with the ruby on his forehead be her husband?

That night, the Princess and her handmaiden went into the garden and hid behind a tree close to the water's edge. On the stroke of midnight, tiny lights began to twinkle on the river, just as they had the night before. Then a stately old man with a long, flowing white beard suddenly rose from the water, dressed in a golden robe and holding a scepter. A young man stood beside the old man's throne, and Fatima recognized him to be her long lost husband. Covering her face with her veil, she left her hiding place and gracefully began to dance along the river. Wild applause greeted her at the end. Then from the throne came a voice: "For such a divine dance, ask us whatever you wish and it shall be granted!"

Fatima tore the veil from her face and cried, "Give me back my husband!"

The old king rose to his feet.

"The King of the Waters of Persia has given his word. Take back your husband, the Ruby Prince. But do not forget how you lost him and be sure that you are more wise in the future!"

The waters opened up once more and then suddenly closed over the King and his court, leaving Fatima and the Ruby Prince behind on the bank, reunited again and happy at last.

The Parrot Shah

Many hundreds of years ago, there once lived a brave young Shah of India. His counselor was a very old and wise man known to many as the Chief Minister called Saleb.

Like all of his subjects, the Shah worshipped the God of Reason. Everyday, he would go to the temple he had built close to the palace in order to worship his God. In response to the Shah's devout and sincere prayers, the God of Reason gave the Shah good advice on the very difficult art of government. Indeed, the kingdom had never been so well ruled and under the Shah's steady and wise rule, it had also become very prosperous, and its people very happy.

One day, at the end of his visit to the temple, the Shah was amazed to hear the God of Reason's deep voice say to him: "You no longer need my advice. You are now wise enough on your own. You can continue to pray to me, but this is the last time you will speak to me. But before I leave you to Fate, I will grant you one wish. Anything you ask will be given to you."

On his knees before the statue of his God, the Shah thought for a very long time before replying. Then he said: "Oh God who rules over us all, thank you for all that you have done for me and for my people these past many years. I would ask that you give me the power to transfer my soul into the body of another man or animal, whenever I would wish it. And let my own body remain intact until such time that I choose to enter it once again."

"It shall be so," said the God. "Now listen carefully . . . ." and the God spoke to the Shah for a very long time.

Back at the palace, the Shah quickly called to his Chief Minister.

"Would you believe it, Saleb! In his infinite goodness, the God has given me his trust and a great power . . . ." and he told his wise counselor of everything that had transpired between him and the God that morning in the temple.

The old man, however, had great doubts about the wisdom of the Shah's action, but he said nothing and hid his feelings from his master.

"This strange incredible thing could change my master's whole life and destiny," the old man said to himself later on that day. "I must do my best to make sure he doesn't alter his ways and make dangerous changes. What he needs is a wife and family to keep him from making any risky decisions. It takes only a few strange deeds to ruin a good and solid government."

Far beyond the mountains bordering on the Shah's kingdom lay a great and fertile plain, the realm of a very old king. This king had an only daughter named Gala.

Gala was young and beautiful and so sweet and gentle that her father hated the thought of letting her go in order to see her get married. The court, however, was eager to see her as a bride. The king was very possessive and wanted to keep Gala all to himself, and with the help of a wizard, he had thought up a plan to discourage her suitors. A magic tree was planted in the garden, a huge pomegranate that had three fruits. At sunset, the branches bent over to touch the ground and the fruit would split open.

Inside each lay a soft feather bed. Gala, the princess, slept in the middle one, with her servants on either side. The fruit closed over the maidens and the branches would swing back up towards the sky, carrying the princess high above all danger.

Seven walls had been built round this magic garden, each one studded with thousands of spikes that nobody could ever hope to cross. The king sent out a proclamation:

"Any man wishing to marry my daughter must be noble, rich and handsome. But he must also succeed in picking the fruit in which the princess sleeps. Yet, if he falters in trying to cross the seven circles of spikes, he will be left to die."

As it so happened, the Shah's Chief Minister decided that the princess would make a good wife for his master. As time went by, many fine brave warriors perished on the spikes guarding the princess's enchanted garden. Saleb, however, was sure that the special divine powers of the Shah would help him to overcome any obstacle.

Saleb wanted to persuade the Shah to try to win the princess's hand. Every day, Saleb would describe in great detail the various trials the suitors had to go through in order to reach the king's only daughter. At the beginning, the Shah was amused by all of the strange stories. Then, gradually, he became curious and began to ask questions about the princess of Saleb himself. The clever Minister told his master of the princess's beauty and all about her many brave suitors. In the end, the Shah began to fall in love with the girl he had never seen, simply by hearing so many stories about her. In no time at all, he began to consider different ways of reaching the magic garden and the special fruit where the princess slept. He shared his ideas for the princess's hand with his Chief Minister, who was delighted to hear of the Shah's plans.

The very next day, the Shah ordered a large, brightly-feathered parrot with a strong beak to be brought to him. He had decided that he would have to use his magic powers to enter the magic garden, and he said this to Saleb:

"My soul is going to enter the body of this parrot, but my lifeless body will stay here. Watch over it day and night until I come back."

After a long prayer to the God of Reason, the Shah then very carefully did everything he had been told to do in order to move into the body of the parrot. Then he fell into a deep sleep. His breathing slowly grew fainter and fainter until finally it died away completely and he lay still upon the bed. Watching worriedly over his master, Saleb saw that the parrot, which had been sitting quietly on its perch, was now flapping its wings wildly.

The parrot suddenly flew out the window and soared into the air. It flew in the direction of the princess's mountain and was able to reach it very quickly. The air was cold and he flapped heavily upward until the highest peak was soon left behind. Far below lay the turrets of the palace and the glinting of many thousands of dangerous spikes. Somehow, the parrot struggled across the rows of sharp steel and landed safely beside the magic tree.

The sun was setting when Gala and her two servants stepped into the fruit to enjoy their rest for the night. As the pomegranates closed around them, the calls of the three maidens rang in the ears of the Parrot Shah, and in the second before they shut completely, he caught a fleeting glimpse of the beautiful princess. Her gleaming dark eyes seemed to smile at him. Then the branches of the tree rose into the air, carrying with it its

precious cargo, and the fruit shrank back to its normal size. As the branches pointed upward, the parrot sprang into the air and, with a blow of his strong beak, ripped the pomegranate containing the princess from its branch. Clutching the fruit in his claws, he flew off into the night.

The twinkling stars lit the Parrot Shah's path home. This time it was even harder to cross the mountain, but the parrot felt neither cold nor fatigue, for he kept within his mind's eye the picture of Gala's lovely face. As he gripped the magic pomegranate, it slowly grew heavier and heavier within his beak. The parrot knew that its weight and bulk was hindering his flight, and his wings grew weary and slow. In a panic, he felt that he was going to drop the fruit, but it was again the thought of Gala's beautiful eyes that alone managed to fill him with new strength.

Suddenly he saw the valley of his home. He was over the mountain. Now, he had only to find enough energy to go on and re-enter his own body. And then admire Gala, the bride of his dreams.

Saleb had been watching from the window ever since his master had left. He stood by the window, which had been left open day and night, and guarded over his master's lifeless body. Full of remorse at having coaxed the Shah into undertaking such a dangerous mission, the poor Minister had never stopped praying. Suddenly, at the sound of wings flapping in the distance, he leapt to his feet:

"Thank Heavens!" he cried. "At last! At last!"

The stars were fading and the sun was slowly beginning to brighten the night sky, tinting the clouds with pink, when the parrot suddenly flew through the window. Gently laying its precious burden upon the bed, the bird went back to its perch, and the Shah's body came slowly to life. Saleb threw himself in front of his master.

"Sire!" he gasped. "I have been so afraid. I thought I would never see you again."

The magic worked as the sun rose over the horizon and its first rays shone through the window. The pomegranate began to grow and grow as it did each morning. Then it gently opened and out stepped Gala, smiling.

"Where am I? How did I get here?" she gasped in surprise, blinking at her strange new surroundings and the two men bowing low before her. The Shah quickly stepped forward and clasped her hand, kissing it fleetingly.

"Gala, you are in your future husband's palace! I have completed your father's task and have safely removed you from his magic garden. Now you are to be my bride and together we will rule this kingdom."

The Chief Minister clapped his hands in delight.

The wedding took place the very next day and the couple ruled happily ever after. From that day on all the parrots in the Shah's kingdom were treated with great respect. A parrot was even included in the royal coat of arms and fluttered from the army's banners, and to all the people in the Shah's land, it became a sacred symbol.